Exploring Doubt

'At a time when the public debate on religious faith seems to be more about conviction and ideology than about doubt and ambiguity, this book offers a personal and often moving account of the value of uncertainty. Alex Wright observes the beauty of the physical landscape and combines observation and reflection with memories of human turmoil. His unfolding narrative will take you gently inside yourself.'

Mona Siddiqui, OBE, Professor of Islamic and Interreligious Studies, University of Edinburgh

'Three braids of enquiry are woven together in this book: an evocative depiction of the north Norfolk landscape; a lingering reflection on the breakup of a marriage; and a theological enquiry into the importance of *not* being certain. What emerges is a profound study of the deep relations that bind place, people and Christian believing. It is as much a composition – the writing poetic, sinuous and subtle – as a study of the fragility, evanescence and spirituality of human belonging. The book is a wonderful and imaginative piece of work that lingers long after it has been put aside and resonates with the authenticity of a true writer's voice.'

Graham Ward, Regius Professor of Divinity, University of Oxford

'John Henry Newman once sought to comfort a bereaved friend by noting how the dead can seem more real to us than when they were alive, more present in their absence than when in the flesh. This apparent paradox – of presence in absence – is the theme of Alex Wright's remarkable book. It is a book of bereavements, personal and cultural. Wright weaves together a set of reflections on the loss and remaining of faith in our times with the loss of his first marriage, setting both in the landscape – the seascape – of the North Norfolk coast. For it was there that his marriage both flowered and faded, in a place where the distinction between land and sea is both lost and remembered in the ceaseless flow of the tides. There is a revelation in the sea's withdrawing, a renewal in the passing of relationships, and it is the finding of such returns that Wright's book delivers: a calm, cultured, beguiling – if sometimes unsettling – meditation that will resonate with many, in many different ways. A wonderful and profound book.'

Gerard Loughlin, Professor of Theology, Durham University

'"Why should the highways and byways of our lives be clearly laid out? Why should our routes and stories be maps that are straightforward to read and decipher? Similarly, why should the boundaries between faith and unbelief be instantly recognizable? The landscapes of longing are not so easily charted or defined." At a time when public discourse about religion in the West seems convulsed between the sterile poles of certainty and atheism, contemporary spiritual writer Alex Wright dares to lift up doubt — not as the opposite of faith, but rather as the path to its deepest heart and greatest transformative potential. Written in beautiful, elegiac prose, the insights of *Exploring Doubt* emerge from a searingly personal, yet recognisably universal, story of loss: of a marriage, a beloved home, and the ancient, mutable landscape of Norfolk in which the author's life was anchored. Instead of pivoting to a sanguine theology of transcendence as a balm, Wright meditates instead on the unceasing change and unknowing that landscape evokes: centuries of coastal lives, the witness of medieval devotion, and the sparkling, ephemeral, yet eternal cycles of the natural world, especially the migratory birds in their homeless flight. This masterful, generous book, richly fed by the wellsprings of both natural and human history, tenderly invites us back to "the places where we have suffered the greatest losses and the most uncertainty" – to flux, doubt, and mystery: all the landscapes our distracted world urges that we avoid – and shows us the brilliant clarity that may paradoxically await us there. *Exploring Doubt* is a prayer for our time.'

Kimberley C. Patton, Professor of the Comparative and Historical Study of Religion, Harvard University

Exploring Doubt

Landscapes of Loss and Longing

Alex Wright

DARTON · LONGMAN + TODD

First published in Great Britain in 2016 by
Darton, Longman and Todd Ltd
1 Spencer Court
140 – 142 Wandsworth High Street
London SW18 4JJ

ISBN 978–0–232–53060–5

A catalogue record for this book is available from the British Library

The author and publisher gratefully acknowledge the following for permission
to reproduce copyright material: From 'Winter Song', Lawrence Sail, *Songs of the
Darkness: Poems for Christmas* (Enitharmon Press, 2010); from 'The First Island',
Kevin Crossley-Holland, *Poems from East Anglia* (Enitharmon Press, 1997); from
'The Wall', Kevin Crossley-Holland, *Poems from East Anglia* (Enitharmon Press,
1997); Psalm 13 (14 lines) from *A Book of Psalms: Selected and Adapted from the
Hebrew* by Stephen Mitchell, copyright © 1993 by Stephen Mitchell, reprinted
by permission of HarperCollins Publishers; Julia Blackburn and the Random
House Group for an extract from *The Leper's Companions*; passages quoted from
'Far Point' by Charles Tomlinson are copyrighted and are reprinted here by kind
permission of Carcanet Press Limited, Manchester, UK. Every effort has been
made to contact the owners of copyright. Should any material appear herein
without permission, the publisher would be glad to make good the oversight in
any future printings or editions of the work.

Phototypeset by Kerrypress, St Albans
Printed and bound in Great Britain by Bell & Bain Ltd., Glasgow

To Joe: companion in adversity

CONTENTS

PREFACE AND ACKNOWLEDGEMENTS

As I have become older my books seem to have become more personal. Perhaps this is a case of age bringing not necessarily sagacity but more in the way of hard knocks: the bruises and scars are simply more prominent and visible than they were, and therefore – rightly or wrongly – felt to be worth giving some attention to. This short book meshes experience with the topic of doubt. It addresses, through the prism of my own recent perspectives on doubt, the significant merit to be attached to the subject, at least as I see it. I wanted to write about doubt and ambiguity because so many of our present discussions about belief and its opposite seem to be dominated by comforting but perhaps ultimately false certainties. One of my aims is to push the 'Certaintists', whether they be atheists or unquestioning believers, out of their comfort zone. Conviction undeniably has its place in life, and many hard decisions require an attitude of positive or single-minded determination to see them through satisfactorily; but as a rule of thumb, doubt is surely a more honest and truthful response to the instabilities and unknowns that life inevitably throws in our direction. Most of the time, we simply don't know what's coming our way, whether cloud or comet; and I am at one with Peter Hitchens when he wryly and drily remarks that 'These days I know with complete certainty that there are a number of things about which I have no idea at all, and nor does anyone else.'[1]

Doubt has not I feel received enough attention, in the difficult business of navigating the white-water rapids of faith and unbelief, as a pragmatic and interpretative category of value. The words of the writer of the Gospel of Luke have sometimes been used as a sort of benchmark, in eliding or associating faith with conviction: '*The Lord said, "If you had faith like a grain of mustard seed, you would tell this sycamore tree, 'Be uprooted, and be planted in the sea,' and it would obey you."*' (17:6) By this reckoning, faith is actually equated with certainty, and it is certainty, not irresolution, that becomes key to unlocking participation in the supposed life to come. The burgeoning certainty of faith can, it seems, move mountains – as well as trees – into the ocean. Nevertheless, for all that it has been made peripheral, or pushed out to the margins, in the officially sanctioned history or dubiously censorial processes of Western religion, doubt – the much more interesting obverse of conviction – has managed to hang on, despite persisting and often determined attempts to extinguish it. Many significant figures in Christian history and spirituality have recognised the extraordinary value of dubiety, and indeed have based their major creative thinking on it. I have tried to indicate in the book why I think that they are right. What follows, then, is written with a theological if not explicitly Christian sensibility; and in that respect I have done my best to engage those – whether believers, uncertain seekers or simply the curious and religiously uncommitted – who hold out for the continuing presence in the world of sacred value, presence and meaning. (It is thus arguably a quintessential book from Darton, Longman and Todd: a publisher that, to its great credit, has never turned aside, in addressing matters of religion, from the sceptic's or agnostic's gaze.)

In tackling my themes, it will be obvious from the start that I owe a great deal to the various writers upon whom I draw; their insights have enabled me, however inadequately or sketchily, to try to paint a picture in broad and impressionistic brushstrokes. These imprecise splodges, which take form and inspiration from the creative and intellectual labour of others, are an implicit admission of my appreciation of the value of a crystalline and Pre-Raphaelite attention to scholarly detail. Errors of fact or judgement are of course nothing to do with others' work, and I take full responsibility for any regrettable misuse or misinterpretation of what they have written and devised. Alongside keener thinkers than I, the landscapes and seascapes of north Norfolk also figure prominently here. This is not just because that part of eastern England was my home for several years, and so comprised the topographical and emotional background to the themes contained and explored in the book; but also because in their own impermanence and elusive character they encapsulate in soil and sand and clay the very ambiguities and ambivalences that I wish to develop in more abstract ways. Norfolk anchors the book to the rich earth especially of a medieval spirituality that remains distinctive and inspiring, and which I would like to share with my readers. Each chapter is prefaced by a range of materials that includes a mix of reflective reminiscences written by me and quotations from apposite (or so I would hope) spiritual-cum-philosophical literature by others; I have tried here to evoke the resonant character of seashore and wide skies that entices people back to the coast time and again.

Since it draws on my own experience, it is also, tangentially and peripherally, about a divorce. That experience – regrettably undergone by people of all ages and places, but in each instance unpredictable and highly individualised in its emotional impact – is in parts of the book used, just as Norfolk is, as a heuristic to explore the wider implications of uncertainty and displacement. It will I hope be clear to the reader from the start that no judgements whatsoever are made about the marriage itself, about where responsibility for its ending lies or about the other party involved. In the first place, it would be wholly inappropriate to do so. I do not wish to cause disquiet or rake over embers now long cold. The book is in any case fundamentally about how a particular encounter with loss and absence may inform and enrich the wider interrogation of doubt and faith, not about the relationship itself – which is in many important and private ways simply inexpressible, resisting any kind of analysis. In the second place, my thoughts towards the other person involved contain a large measure of fellow feeling: no one, even if they might think that they will, comes out of a divorce unbloodied or unscathed, and the consequences of that can only evoke commonality. My hope – since she knows herself how valuable and insightful experiential theology can be – is that my former spouse might forgive the use made of my experience as a fruitful platform for broader religious and spiritual reflection. So as to be authentic, and real, and since the emotional impact of marital rupture was for me considerable, the encounter with separation and the doubts that that induced can only be written about in a way that presupposes at least some degree of personal engagement. It is my further hope that this articulation of absence, fragmentation and recovery might give some solace, or at least distraction, to those persons of either gender who themselves have gone through the miserable business of splitting up. If the book achieves that, it will have been worth writing indeed.

Even a short book like this incurs many debts. To my editor at DLT, David Moloney, I owe inestimable gratitude for his support and encouragement even when it looked as if the varied pressures of life and work might prevent the book appearing at all. I thank him most warmly and gratefully, as also his colleagues Will Parkes and Helen Porter for their sterling work on, respectively, marketing and production. I appreciate the opportunity that John and Margaret Bowker gave me to explore some of these ideas in a very preliminary way in their theological workshop at Hengrave Hall in Suffolk in 2002. I am grateful too to my colleagues at I.B.Tauris, especially Iradj Bagherzade and Jonathan McDonnell, for their encouragement and good humour (including Iradj's doubts about doubt!), and for providing a congenial publishing home where, over the years, I have been able to express myself in an eclectic manner across disciplines and between genres that has perhaps at times surprised them as much as it has me. A number of people either offered acute suggestions in conversation, or else agreed to read the text in advance of publication; in this regard I must thank Graham Ward, Mona Siddiqui, Gerard Loughlin, Eddie Howells and Kimberley Patton. At the November 2015 American Academy of Religion meetings in Atlanta, Kimberley gave me the impetus, encouragement and advice that I needed to get back to the text with renewed vigour and self-belief. I count myself fortunate to be her friend as well as her publisher; indeed, without her timely pep-talk the book may not have crossed the finishing line. Other friends too have been inspirational, and the book is dedicated to Joseph Ashley with whom I shared the worst of times that I now realise were also, paradoxically, the best of times. At different moments, Rebecca Levene, Laurence Hallam, Alison Lawson, Clare Martelli and Alice Orton were veritable cantilevers of load-bearing weight, offering fortification over the occasional lunch, drink or dinner. The Italian community in Oxford has, in its turn and over the last several years, provided distraction and a great deal of support, and in this regard I must express my thanks to lovely sisters from the Marche, Giovanna and Paola Ferrante, to Sara Girardello and to (honorary Italian) Thomas Wright (not of course forgetting – last but certainly not least – the irrepressibly exuberant Lola), for their humour, solidarity, friendship and splendid *cucina italiana*. My family, especially my mother and father, offered much encouragement and practical advice and did their best to help me get through the dark days. That my father and stepmother were able to attend my wedding in Padua, despite dad's illness, is something for which I will be forever grateful.

Above all, Mara Violato has shown me that no amount of doubt or debate about which *pastina* is best at Tonolo (that famous Dorsoduro institution) can substitute for the love of a good woman – which she is, and a great deal more besides. No form of conventional thanks from me could do justice to what I owe her.

INTRODUCTION: ARRIVAL

'This is the land's salt edge
which must not be transgressed –
the tides that mull by a bare crescent,
the damp mantle of mist.'
– Lawrence Sail, 'Winter Song'

'So the boat came for us. The island stretched out to
us and we took it for granted. And no one asked by
Which creeks we had come or could return.'
– Kevin Crossley-Holland, 'The First Island'

'Now falls the night of the world: – O Spirit moving upon
the waters
Your peace instil
In the animal heat and splendour of the blood
The hot gold of the sun that flames in the night
And knows not down-going
But moves with the revolutions in the heavens.'
– Edith Sitwell

This coast forever echoes. One cannot get away from
memory. It has seeped so far down into the layers of
chalk and sand and flint that the earth is running with it,
like water from a river's source. Or blood from a wound
that cannot be staunched. Following those frontiersmen
from the continent, who were bold enough to cross wide
channels roaring between cliffs now scoured by ice-
melt, the Romans came. They set up camp at Holme
and Branodunum, fortifying their timber outposts with
garrison and stockade. They built roads and fine villas,
fished for oysters in the mudflats, and ran their muscular

horses on the strandline. Some say the Dalmatian cavalry were based here and that stallions from a far-flung homeland raced each other across the sands – fierce animals moulded from ivory, bone and quicksilver, as swift as the dangerous north wind that dances down from Iceland.

I walk out to the Island across the gleaming sands of Holkham beach. Ahead of me the sun scorches the sky like a magnesium flare while corkscrewing, twisting sand devils unforgivingly whip and flail at my unprotected legs. I can feel it all around and behind me: the sinuously winding creaks; the mudflats reflecting a burning sky; the coastal reedbeds and gorse-covered heaths. This is my country. Scattered along the strandline are mermaid's purses, razorshells and dismembered pieces of starfish – the graveyard of an unforgiving coast. Oystercatchers and curlews pick their way gingerly through driftwood and bladderwrack, as if trying to map a safe route through wave and spume. Behind me the grey-silver marram dances and sways in graceful valediction of some secret cause, while away and beyond at the horizon the capriciously changeable breakers, placid as glass, caress the land they touch; flecked with aquamarine, violet and indigo, today they only hint at the fury they can contain.

Mud and clay, dune and saltmarsh, rain and sun: the coast of my life's love calls to me. I can smell the salt on the breeze, as congregations of birds wheel and soar above me: shelducks and pink-footed geese gathering to watch the winter sun set. The solstice tides rise and fall, slow and flow – flow and slow – moving rhythmically now as if in syncopated sympathy with my own heart and pulse-beat.

If you were to look out across the fields of meadowland between the north Norfolk villages of Cley and Wiveton, it might be hard to fathom that six centuries ago this pastoral setting, bisected by the meandering River Glaven, was one of the great ports of England. But if you closed your eyes and imagined these bucolic fields and meadows before you inundated now with water, many millions of cubic feet of it, then you would perhaps have a better sense of how completely seascape has been transformed into landscape. Improbable as it seems, medieval Cley (which retains its moniker 'Next-the-Sea', though its beach is now a mile distant from the village) was a great international trading centre. The mariners of coastal Cley voyaged as far as Scandinavia and the Hanseatic towns of the Baltic. Local produce of wool, barley, oats, malt and oysters were exported there; and the Norfolk men returned with wines, fine cloth and spices. Trade with the Low Countries was important too – and continental influence may still be seen all over this part of the coast in the form of the ubiquitous Dutch gable. Wood and madder arrived from Picardy, armour from Germany, while from Norway came 'greywork', the fur of the arctic squirrel caught in winter and highly prized by both court and aristocracy. Fishing too was a vital industry. Sailors went to Iceland and back, oyster beds were worked for trade with London and lobsters and crabs were harvested from the inshore waters.

Cley and Wiveton are haunted by a ghostly topography that endures in the monuments and artefacts their ports have left behind. These quiet meadows have later been superimposed on top of a massive, bustling harbour which – along with doomed towns like Shipden and Dunwich – is part of the lost Atlantis of England's eastern counties. The substantial circular iron bands once to be seen hammered into the side of Wiveton Church (and still within touching distance of local reminiscence) were fixed there not for show or aesthetic decoration, but rather to tether ships of a hundred tons or more at anchor.[1] For this Arcadian floodplain was in the Middle Ages an estuary up to three-quarters of a kilometre wide;[2]

deluged with seawater at high tide, its wind-lashed surface would have lapped the bottom of the churchyard wall. On the other side of the meadow, the great grey bulk of St Margaret's of Antioch – a far larger and more imposing building than one might have expected to find in a small village like Cley – testifies to the wealth and financial power of a thriving but now poignantly vanished sea-trade. The sunken moorings of this busy delta were haven then to a dipping armada, its forest of pennants straining into the breeze and fluttering in bold heraldic symphony. Concerto of cinnabars and whites, of aquas, yellows and viridescent greens, the unfurling sails of tacking and close manoeuvring medieval cogs, surrounded by countless smaller craft, would have been as stirring a sight as any to be found on England's coast. The peaceful lawns of Newgate Green, just in front of St Margaret's, once were sandbanks where traders and sailors would haul in their oars and beach their boats. If you closed your eyes again you might imagine that you can hear the mariners hailing each other across the bay, exchanging good-natured greetings and ribald curses as they begin to unload from their craft their brimming cargoes of oats and oysters.[3]

North Norfolk is full of memories. Its soil is compacted with the past and its residue. And this is a book in part about the significance of memory, particularly as it relates to notions of home and place and landscape. But it is also about leaving, and loss and above all uncertainty. Current debates, many of them anguished, about tides of migration from the Middle East have forced many of us to think more carefully about what constitutes a legitimate 'home' – as has the increase of unpredictable weather events precipitated by climatic change and the recent misery of flooding. Nothing seems as secure as it did; nothing is as dependable as it was; little is certain as the twenty-first century moves towards early maturity. But without in any way wishing to minimise the personal agony of homelessness and displacement, or individual

4

sufferings caused by water inundation, it is perhaps worth asking if wider uncertainty is necessarily the evil it might at first seem. Some years ago the unexpected collapse of my marriage forced me to move away from Norfolk, a place invested for me with numerous dreams and aspirations. I miss that incomparable landscape every day. I miss the life and wife that I had. But that process of leaving, of 'moving on', of the good things that came to me afterwards and unexpectedly, would not have come into being at all had I not had to face the trauma and fear of uprooting. In chaos and ruin actually lay opportunity, even if at the time I had little clear sense of purpose, direction or even of meaning.

Often our pathways are hidden from us, and the roads that diverge in the wood seem not so much choices made as enforced and reluctant tramps into foliage that from the perimeter of the forest looks distinctly dark and uninviting. But dank and unfamiliar woodland may yet reveal surprises: perhaps there is concealed vegetation growing there that we have never encountered before – mosses, flowers and funguses of startling variety; or there are pleasant and shady hollows to be found in which, but for necessity, we might never otherwise have been able to rest. Landscapes can be cherished beyond reckoning, and for some of us the loss of them may mean a permanent sense of exile; but they can also, at times, seem too close or overly-predictable in their familiarity – and it is then that removal and difference may be not only enriching but also liberating. The Czech novelist Milan Kundera writes wisely and with deep personal engagement about the ambivalence of exile. Speaking of Odysseus, whom he uses as an astute example, Kundera remarks that for twenty years he – that is Odysseus – 'had thought about nothing but his return. But once he was back, he was amazed to realise that his life, the very essence of his life, its centre, its treasure, lay outside Ithaca, in the twenty years of his wanderings.'[4] This is a theme – uncertainty about place and belonging, and the richness of doubt that accompanies change – that I will develop and expand later in the book.

One of the joys of living in Norfolk – whose landscapes lack the epic scale of Cumbria or Scotland, or the mythic drama of Cornwall or Wales, but which are nevertheless uniquely and integrally related to its mutating shoreline – is the persistent sense that you are standing on top of history, or participating in a story whose beginnings go back many centuries. Sometimes, however, you have to look carefully – underneath the surface – to see how and where the narrative has unfolded. This is not a topography which shouts about its charms, and is perhaps the more interesting for that. It is an elusive landscape that you have to take your time to get to know; and it is only then that its secrets are gradually and grudgingly divulged. Beyond the coastal road at Holkham now lie water meadows, pinewoods and then dune and marram grass; a brisk twenty minute walk might get you to the sea. But in the Middle Ages that coastal road marked the shoreline, and now landlocked Holkham was a small but busy harbour that received both fishing boats and trading ships. The sea has long retreated, and the lineation of the coast has altered. This is a deceptive border whose exact boundaries are never entirely certain, never entirely dependable. Those who live here know that, while warm spring weather might be found a mere couple of miles inland, on the coast meanwhile the horizon may be shrouded in the blanketing and deadening layers of a sea-fog that has drifted in, wraith-like and phantasmagorically, from across invisible and silent waters. The unpredictable sea-frets of the north Norfolk coast, which sometimes vanish as quickly as they materialise, are a perfect symbol for the way the changing shoreline has itself enigmatically shape-shifted over the centuries.

Once the agricultural powerhouse of England, the economic importance of Norfolk declined after it was bypassed by the Industrial Revolution. It is now a land of secrets, of covert places and of communities lost after the devastation of the Black Death. One of the most remarkable memorials to the many abandoned villages of the county is St Mary's at Houghton-on-the-Hill.[5] This lonely church is the last survivor of a once thriving medieval hamlet which succumbed to the plague of 1348–49. Now a solitary and abandoned outpost, standing improbably in the middle of a field, St Mary's was at one time filled with the hubbub of the villagers, and illuminated by many candles as light flickered over the delicate red lead and white vermilion traceries of the church's Norman frescoes. It is no accident that one of the most significant of the remarkable images uncovered in this ancient building depicts a wheel of fortune: a popular medieval motif used to illustrate the ups and downs of day-to-day existence. This was not the expression of a religious sensibility that denied or underplayed the unfairness of fate; rather one that tried to make sense of it. Here was no simplistic portrayal of an easy faith; rather a brilliant artistic interpretation that acknowledged in full that life could be unpredictable, deadly and capricious. Uncertainty about what was to come, in this life or the next – when the worshipper might just as easily be prodded by demons towards hell as set on the road to salvation – was an essential component of the lively hubbub of village worship and conversation. Confronted by the solemn saints, and the faces of the damned and elect that coolly return our gaze after the passing of many centuries, we are able to enter imaginatively into a system of belief that was this society's heartbeat. It was also a belief that fully accommodated doubt.

Far from being the forlorn and forsaken outposts they resemble today, rural churches like St Mary's were at one time the barometers of their societies' health. They offered sustenance at times of great hardship and – such as during the Black Death – distress. But they were also gathering places for the whole community where the realities of life and death could be represented pictorially, enabling everyone to share the essential truth of their own experience. The people who constructed this building, who filled it with light and sympathy and lively discussion, are long gone. What they have left are echoes in the dark. But here is a concrete reminder, too, that faith in pre-Reformation England mattered because it was rooted in the very soil of the community. This was no abstract codex, existing in isolation from what was happening in the fields and streets and on the deathbed. It depicted a suffering and a loss that worshippers would have known for themselves all too keenly. A richly decorated interior, with wall paintings illustrating the Last Judgment, the lush flora of the Garden of Eden and Noah's Ark tossed on the stormy waters of a glowering sea, allowed everyone to share not only in worship but also in the collegial coming together of everyday social concerns. This church not only served the community; in a profound and important sense it *was* the community.

It is a natural human urge to want to hold onto what we cannot. But like Holkham and the Glaven Ports, our existence is governed by the grains of time. The natural sand accumulations brought in by the ebb and flow of the tide have been the death of the ancient trading harbours of Wiveton, Blakeney, Cley and its satellite settlement of Salthouse. Similarly, the best laid plans of life have a way of being blown off course. Illness can strike suddenly. The parents who were once so hale no longer seem physically robust. The siblings to whom we once were close have grown away from us. The spouse whom once we loved is long gone. The world we inhabited can be recalled in memory only, just as the church of St Mary's at Houghton recalls a village long since lost. It is then that a coast in constant flux becomes a symbol whose veracity we can understand in both head and heart.

The more time that I spent on the Norfolk coast the more I understood that this is a geography shaped by change. Sea has become land. Land has been reclaimed by sea. The famous Seahenge, dug up on a beach at Holme-next-the Sea in 1998, was once situated some distance inland.[6] It was built four thousand years ago on the edge of an ancient forest of birch, oak, elm, hazel and lime. Though the landscape around the mysterious timber circle has shape-shifted and morphed, being 'backswamp' – technically dryland, but consistently very wet – it has nevertheless always been a place in continuous transition, where the boundaries between sea and land were never fixed or solid.[7] Round the coast, to the east, the depredations of the waves have likewise chipped away at the cliffs and bluffs of Happisburgh. Like Suffolk's Dunwich and Cromer's Shipden it will eventually succumb to Neptune's rage; in the end it will exist only in recollection, story and in the form of old maps. That fundamental change in soil and strand, loam and stone, is mirrored by the unpredictable patterns of our own lives. We might long for security and longevity but these are the very things our own mortality denies us. We are creatures made of light and gossamer; sailors on the seas of fate and chance.

Time spent in a much loved landscape being battered by erosion, and the permanent threat of land loss, becomes a metaphor for the wider forfeit of the things and people we love and yet are often forced by life's vicissitudes to relinquish. The seemingly solid ground beneath our feet might crumble away at any moment. But often there is hope, even in the darkest and most unstable of places. Scattered along the north Norfolk coast are a string of churches that serve as sanctuaries to an often beleaguered seaside community. St Nicholas at Salthouse, for example, standing on its promontory above the shoreline, is visible for miles around. Like a lighthouse, it is a beacon not just of hope but of endurance. Just as St Mary's has, it has survived both time and tide. This prompts us to a realisation that these venerable churches, marooned by the centuries in volatile landscapes that actively seek their destruction, speak of something that is nevertheless significant. Would the certainty of their survival – something increasingly unlikely as the sea defences of Salthouse are finally abandoned – in fact detract from the nobility and dignity of their own mortality? Is an eternal endlessness, an ongoing existence unthreatened by wave and storm and disconnected from the lives of those who inhabit these settlements, preferable to a time-limitedness anchored in mutability? Communities like Shipden, Dunwich and Happisburgh may fail as they are swallowed by the hungry ocean. But in so doing are they not mirroring our own journey through the volatile landscape of instability and doubt? Death, divorce, terminations of whatever kind – sometimes desperately sad, often unexpectedly sudden – help us to realise that nothing is certain: neither faith, nor life. And yet in the midst of endings there are new beginnings: the hidden flower in the rock crevice; the marram grass on the lonely dune. The end is not always absolute but may contain within it the seed of transformation, however difficult it may be to see or determine at the moment of dissolution.

In the landscapes that shape and surround us we recognise much that is familiar; but there is much here too that is hidden from us. In the early Carboniferous (362–290 million years ago), Britain drifted north of the equator and was then engulfed by a tropical sea teeming with marine life. In the late Cretaceous (145–65 million years ago), the country was submerged again and vast chalk beds were formed out of the shells of microscopic plankton – organisms floating on the sparkling surface of another vanished and sun-scorched ocean. The chalk of north Norfolk's Wiveton Down is a maritime, not a terrine, product. Similarly, clear chalk streams like the Nar, Stiffkey and Glaven are the direct result of the titanic motion of continents: grand and monumental movements taking place and shape over vast aeons of time, and within a chronology almost inconceivable by human reckoning. The now firm ground beneath us was once the submerged floor of a seabed. The interchange of sea and land in Norfolk is thus a process that goes back more than just centuries. Transition, in both landscape and life, is as inevitable as the process of ageing itself.

In such indeterminacy there is room not only for grief at that which is lost but also for wonder at that which may be reconstituted. Beneath the wide skies of Norfolk it is entirely possible to feel the weight of loneliness and insignificance descend. These are skies whose immensity brings you face to face with the probability of your own nugatory existence. Yet in the very inconsequentiality of who and what we are, there is scope also for fascination with, even celebration of, that which we do not know and can never properly understand. For example, we do not know the meaning of Seahenge at Holme-next-the-Sea, or why it was built. Thanks to carbon dating we do know with remarkable exactitude in which year the central oak tree of the site was felled (2050 BC), and even which season the felling was done (between April and June).[8] What we do not and cannot understand is what purpose it served or what symbolic or ritual function it had. This inverted oak stump, buried upside down in a peat bed by its early Bronze Age makers – offering what the archaeologist Francis Pryor calls 'a compelling ... frightening and eerie image'[9] – almost certainly had wider symbolic significance. It may have represented vital forces being returned to the earth, the source of all life. Constructed of timber, it may have been a shrine to the trees themselves. But as Pryor says, we cannot 'read' its specific meaning, 'any more than we can "read" the meaning of a religious service'.[10] Some secrets that are buried underground resist interpretation, and are all the more captivating and powerful in consequence. In presenting us with the echoes, still discernible over countless centuries, of a world and civilisation now long-lost, they exert the pull over us of the numinous and incomprehensible.

It is just such recognition of the changing and elusive character of landscape, and the mystery of what it contains, which prompts Andrew Brown, one of the best writers on religion at the *Guardian*, to reflect in another wilderness context on the meditative power located in impermanence: 'Beneath that sky', Brown writes, 'I didn't feel small. I felt transient. I knew I would flicker away soon like everything else, a swallow, or a grayling, or one of the large, cautious ants on the edge of the road … Twelve thousand years ago the whole valley was bare rock pressed in the grinding darkness underneath a glacier; one day, the river would vanish again … Long before that I would die. I'd be as dead as the grayling I had eaten by the river; as dead as anyone I'd loved; everyone I could even remember. Everyone who could ever remember me would die. I didn't want anything else. Up against that huge sky, there was nothing else to want. But this wasn't a revelation for my benefit: there would never be an apocalypse or a reason. It just was'.[11] Transience, as this writer rightly implies, is not synonymous with either nihilism or emptiness. It should not lead inevitably to despair. Neither does the very fact of being, of existing, necessarily pose either a question or an answer. It simply is: the alpha and the omega. Brevity and instability, in life and landscape, may even be the start – like the dazzling and unforeseen emergence of Seahenge – of something revelatory. As the *Tao Te Ching* succinctly puts it, the nameless is the beginning of heaven and earth; the named is the mother of ten thousand things. It is that which is nameless, unfathomable, in fact – that about which we can never completely be sure or certain – which fully challenges us as finite creatures, and which perhaps best expresses our capacity to grow and develop as human beings.

In the chapters that follow, I want to explore the fundamental idea that it is in hiddenness, not transparency, that life's meanings may most eloquently be expressed. It is in doubt, not certainty, that we are led towards a proper sense of our true worth and humanity. Drawing on a variety of cultural texts – as well as my own experience over the last few years of termination and abandonment – I will try in addition to show how and why the language of fluidity and provisionality has been, and has to be, the lifeblood of any mature sense of the transcendent. Not only are irresolution and scepticism part of a healthy approach to understanding the world and its mysteries, they are vital to a clearer appreciation that there are limits to all forms of human knowledge and perception. We may perceive that we are part of something 'larger' than ourselves – something benign and something sentient. But we have no capacity to articulate that sensibility in anything other than the language of metaphor, poetry and simile. Putting boundaries around faith – wanting to poke one's finger into the wounded side of Christ, if you like – merely serves to cut us off from the essential mystery that something is happening there which is fundamentally resistant to conviction.

Pascal thought God was to be found most truly in a sense of his absence, not of his presence, and yet this philosopher could still assert: it is not certain that everything is uncertain. For Bonhoeffer, the future of faith famously lay in a religionless Christianity. Simone Weil wrote in similarly elusive and tantalising terms that God is always most present in his emptiness. This is a book about trying to find God in precisely those shadows: in the hidden, sometimes overlooked corners where one might least expect to find him. It is also a book about discovering hope in unexpected places: in a sense of renewal even as one picks one's way gingerly over the ruins of an old life. And of finding traces of wildflowers emerging in-between the cracks of Ground Zero. I hope along the way to have pertinent things to say about current debates about the place of religion in public life, even as I discuss the rich and varied ways in which answers to the 'the big questions' – questions about faith, belief, authenticity and the existence of 'something else' – have always been most effectively articulated through the language not of absolute conviction, but of the marvellously improbable and incredible.

Chapter One

CERTAINTY

'O God, help us not to despise or oppose what we do not understand.'

– William Penn

She is so far away from me; I cannot reach her. I am a bystander in my own play – no longer an actor, but a player backstage whose lines have been forgotten. The real drama, of days being lived, is happening somewhere else. How can happiness so comprehensively drain away? We spoke, but always there were silences behind our words. And then the words ran out. What was unsaid acquired a larger, harder meaning. All the love and laughter evaporated like haze burning off in the morning sun. I try to remember you as you were, as we were, as we walked easily through heath and hill and woodland. So many plans: so many years to plan for. Now I cannot properly see your face. Fragments of joy snatched from illusion. This is what I now hold in my hands: the shattered shards of our life.

'Come over for coffee to see us', they say: 'We want to

be in touch with you.' So I go to visit my wife's parents, who are soon to by my ex-wife's parents, and all too soon I will not be visiting them any longer, at all, indeed ever again: though just weeks before I have been addressed as I always have been, as the 'favourite son-in-law'. I knock, am admitted and step through into their narrow hallway, to be ushered into the living room where an unyielding sofa seems actively to resist the backsides lowered onto it. The faces of my hosts, the faces of my erstwhile Norfolk family, are similarly rigid. Ten feet lie between us: but after the earthquake we might as well be separated by a universe. Desultory chitchat proves too much, even for those schooled for decades in distracting small talk. 'So she has gone away', I say. 'I don't understand.' It's then that I see it; or rather do not see what I always do, and have come to take absolutely for granted on my regular visits to this unassuming but dignified bungalow. The large photograph placed prominently on the mantelpiece for five years, emblematic as some ancient icon, declaratory of parental pride in a bride's joy – the wedding portrait of the two of us – has been removed. That corner of the room feels haunted by a ghost, the shadow of what was and is suddenly, shockingly, no more. 'We still want to see you', my parents-in-law awkwardly announce, before an appalled silence – that of tacitly acknowledged loss – threatens to overwhelm us all in its asphyxiating, splintering finality. But the vanished image suggests otherwise. Where once there was a presence, now there is just absence – the sense of a door not opening to new possibilities but already firmly closed. I make my excuses and leave. Weary, driving home along the coast road, I have to screw up my inconveniently stinging eyes against the low winter sunlight.

'The tree which moves some to tears of joy is in the eyes of others only a green thing which stands in the way.'
– William Blake

'God is in thy heart, yet thou searchest for him in the wilderness.'

– Granth

'Relentless, the sea rolls down from the Pole.
It levelled the dunes last year, removed the marram grass,
Clashed its steel symbols over marsh and macadam.
It attacked me and undermined me; I sway
Like a drunkard now; yet it could not gash me
With its gleaming scythes; it was not strong enough.'
– Kevin Crossley-Holland, 'The Wall'

Whatever we think about religion or God, or the lack of God, perhaps the one certain thing is this: that in discussions about what we do and do not believe in these matters there is simply too much certainty. A sort of dazed and confused sightlessness has arisen, where people stumble around – just as they do in a disintegrating marriage – in the foggy darkness of their mutual lack of comprehension. People of faith are dismissed as fantasists by those who think that any talk of the transcendent has no more significance than a fairy-tale; while those unwilling to reduce all talk of religion to self-indulgent fictionalising are more often than not repelled by what they see in secularists as either a brittle lack of creative imagination or an alarming absence of moral compass.

Much public debate about religion has become a thoroughly regrettable exercise in mud-slinging, where the nuances both of faith and unbelief have become utterly lost in a cacophony of we are right and you are not. The case for atheism is often presented in a way that is crude, simplistic and theologically and historically shaky. On the one hand, many atheists and unbelieving humanists seem unaware that their ideas are much more rooted in Christianity and the Judaeo-Christian tradition than they appreciate themselves. On the other hand, fundamentalism and hostile exclusivism, of whatever faith or persuasion, is generally as unattractive, astringent and lacking in critical self-awareness as its mirror opposite. At a time when how and what people believe is of far more than just academic interest (as we can see from the perils of religious, especially Islamist, radicalisation and of knee-jerk Western prejudice against Islam), the case for more nuanced and generous thinking about religion has never been more urgent or essential. Islam is not some monolithic thing, where all its adherents believe exactly the same thing, just as Christianity embraces enormous subtleties and differences of history and tradition. The contemplative mystical complexities of Sufism, for example, are about as far as it is possible to get from the unyielding literalism of Salafism, while there are large divergences within Christianity in the degree to which, for instance, popular folk and pagan elements feature within and have been incorporated into it.[1] All too often these nuances and shades of grey get lost in black-and-white modern discussions about belief, and the temptation is thus to forget that meaningful and true religion has always involved doubtful interrogation as well as the recitation of credos and creeds. The true divide, as Tina Beattie has recognised,[2] is perhaps no longer between religious believers and those who reject religion, but rather between those who want to use force to twist or pervert religiosity for their own ends and those who want to seek peace and justice in the world whether from a religious or an unbelieving perspective. We require an ongoing conversation of generosity and equality – one that listens to what the other side is saying rather than just shouts about its own virtues, and which recognises that neither party has all the right answers. As a contribution to such discussion I want to argue in what follows for the value of agnosticism, for a recognition of the value of mystery and ambiguity: I want to make a case, and in so doing draw on my own experience (in order to give some personal context to ideas that might otherwise seem a tad too abstract), that sometimes what we do not know is as important as what we do.

The challenging times we live in have undoubtedly led to unhelpful polarisations and fairly unsubtle dichotomising. The so-called New Atheists, among whom Richard Dawkins and the late Christopher Hitchens are perhaps the best known and most prominent voices, have characterised all expressions of religion as at best deluded and factually wrong and at worst deeply harmful. In the new preface to the paperback edition of his famous and hugely successful bestseller *The God Delusion*, Dawkins writes as follows: 'The melancholy truth is that understated, decent, revisionist religion is numerically negligible. To the vast majority of believers around the world, religion all too closely resembles what you hear from the likes of Robertson, Falwell or Haggard, Osama bin Laden or the Ayatollah Khomeini. These are not straw men, they are all too influential, and everybody in the modern world has to deal with them'.[3] For Dawkins, whose adherence to an exclusivist mantra of gradualist natural selection renders talk of God intellectually dishonest ('self-indulgent, thought-denying skyhookery',[4] as he puts it), religious belief is characterised as intrinsically anti-intellectual as well as predisposed – at least in terms of its global impact – to fundamentalism. Dawkins' well-publicised antagonism to religion arises not just from his knowing it to be a delusional and thoroughly discredited way of thinking but also from his dismay at its effects. The inculcation of a religious sensibility in a child by a believing parent is for him even worse than, for example, the institutionalised scandal of child sexual abuse in the Catholic Church: 'Faith can be very dangerous, and deliberately to implant it into the vulnerable mind of an innocent child is a grievous wrong'.[5] Likewise, the conscription of what he calls 'the unprotected child' for physically and psychologically damaging religious purposes is for Christopher Hitchens 'something that even the most dedicated secularist can safely describe as a sin.'[6] As the title of his book suggests that it might, Hitchens reserves his heaviest fire for Islam.[7] Though openly contemptuous of and hostile towards all religions, he remarks that 'it has, however, been some time since Judaism and Christianity resorted openly to torture and censorship.'[8] The Islamic faith, however, remains singularly brutal: 'Not only did Islam begin by condemning all doubters to eternal fire', he writes, 'but it still claims the right to do so in all its dominions, and still preaches that these same dominions can and must be extended by war.'[9] He continues: 'Only in Islam has there been no reformation, and to this day any vernacular version of the Koran must still be printed with a parallel Arabic text.' As Hitchens sees it, 'this ought to arouse suspicion in even the slowest mind.'[10] Though some of his own recent remarks about Muslims and Islam have drawn fire,[11] the truth is that Richard Dawkins, by contrast, has never been discriminatory towards any particular religion at the expense of others, or seemingly singled out any one faith for special belittling or opprobrium. The charge made against him of particularised Islamophobia seems forced to me. One thing that is fully consistent about him is his unwavering hostility to all forms of religious subscription. Indeed, his antipathy towards religious belief of whatever sort might be called thoroughly inclusive and impressively egalitarian. Though a polemicist, and often just as shaky on the rich history of doctrine and belief, he is generally speaking a less offensive atheist than Hitchens.

Whatever one thinks of Dawkins' philosophical and biological arguments about the non-existence of God (and since whole lakes of ink have been spilled over them, whether in defence of his positions or otherwise, I shall not reprise them here[12]), his charge that religion does actual and huge damage in the world finds particular currency at the present moment. (I focus on Dawkins rather than Hitchens because, next to the latter, even Dawkins' thunderous denunciations begin to look like deft Lambeth Palace diplomacy.) This is a context where, on the one hand, creationists in the USA can suppress the teaching in schools of Darwin's writings on evolution (and every five years have significant input into selecting the GOP candidate for President) while, on the other hand, ISIS fighters are massacring the members of any religion (notably Christians, Yezidis and Shia Muslims) who do not adhere to their own ideological, heavily reductionist and Salafist interpretation of Sunni Islam. It is not so surprising that Dawkins' indictment of factual inerrancy and moral bankruptcy often seems to stick to religion when the brittle monotone of jihadist scriptural literalism – manifested in its most extreme form in visceral beheadings of astonishing brutality – is elided, or at least associated, with a Christian biblical fundamentalism which can warp the thinking of young Americans into a misplaced and false counter-culturalism.

There is little doubt that religion in the wrong hands can indeed be deeply destructive. It is hard for me now to look at pictures of the remarkable Temple of Baal in Palmyra, before it was blown up by ISIS, without experiencing a sickening jolt: the certain knowledge that this wonderful building, part of a site hugely significant not only for understanding classical civilisation but the legacy of humanity as a whole, is – thanks to the iconoclastic urges of a thuggish and basically brainwashed cult – no more. John Curtis and others have rightly argued that much more should have been done to save the buildings of Palmyra, and especially the Temple.[13] This monument was one of the most astonishing remnants of the polytheistic classical world.[14] Yet the human cost of unchecked fundamentalism and jihadism has been even more distressing: just for example, ancient communities of Yezidis displaced and killed, their wives and daughters forced into sexual slavery; the longstanding Christian population of Mosul pushed into frantic exile;

and the keeper of antiquities in Palmyra, Khaled Al-Assad, beheaded while defending his site and its treasures, with extraordinary courage, from the depredations of those determined to wreak vengeance on a vanished and harmless paganism. Meanwhile, out on the 2016 presidential campaign trail, one divisive Republican candidate thinks can win votes from conservatives, among them many evangelical conservatives, by proposing – preposterously – that an embargo be put on the travel to the US of all Muslim believers.[15] God is not great, indeed.

But does the certainty of fundamentalists, of whatever persuasion, mean that we should accept the corresponding certainty of the New Atheists and their followers that all forms of belief are in the end malign, threatening or wrong? The danger of this position is that it is in its own way as brittle and unaccommodating as its opposite. Islamophobia, which is on the march in the UK, thrives on the notion that all Muslims are somehow potential ISIS converts: a gullible fifth column just waiting for an excuse to slip away, via covert routes through Turkey, to the purity of a life lived in the spiritually cleansed Islamic Caliphate of Raqqa. This is of course nonsense. The vast majority of those who call themselves 'Muslim' in Britain are as aspirational and non-ideological as their non-Muslim compatriots; they simply want to be allowed to get on with their lives while grappling with the same issues – family, schooling, sex and marriage, ageing, caring for elderly parents, work, retirement, redundancy and so on – that everyone has to deal with, however inadequately and provisionally, on a day-to-day basis. However, this is now a febrile and digital world where 24-hour news is continuously recycled, chewed over, dissected, tweeted, re-tweeted, facebooked and instagrammed. In the ensuing babel of competing media platforms it is hard to make space for subtlety; the loudest and most strident voices are often the ones that receive the most attention. There is something in the charge that the certainty of the sceptics about religion, especially in attributing most of the woes of the world to religious belief (as Dawkins and Hitchens certainly do), has added to the problematic dichotomisation between faith and its opposite. We have reached a climate where the sceptics can only conceive of religion as a poison lying deep within the lymphatic system of human society and culture. According to this view, it often and potently destroys its host, through almost continuous irruptions of violence, intolerance and ignorance, while at other times it is latent, waiting to lure new and naïve generations into its deceptive maze of bigotry and received fantasy.

There is a certain irony in the certainty of the militant secularists (who include many New Atheists) about the deleterious effects of religion, given the origins of secularism itself. Many of the founding fathers of natural science and liberal ideology – such as John Locke – were quite explicit about the Christian theological basis of their ideas; while Immanuel Kant never saw a clash between religious commitment and his progressive philosophy of reason.[16] Graeme Smith, for one, has argued that today's secularism is actually the latest expression of an ever-changing form of Christian belief: 'Secularism in the West is a new manifestation of Christianity', he writes, 'but one that is not immediately obvious because it lacks the usual scaffolding we associate with the Christian religion'.[17] As Smith rightly says, Christianity has always had a fluid and changing identity; it has never been static or ossified into statuary. For this reason, as he puts it well, 'You cannot talk about the essential core of Christian belief, and be understood, without employing the local language'.[18] Context and circumstance, in other words, are all. Truth may be eternal; but it is no good talking about it to the woman or man on the Clapham omnibus in the grammar and syntax of Bethlehem. In other words, religion is a product of culture. How the divine is conceived and articulated is dependent on the human tools available.

It is this sense of the varieties and changing situations of context which tends to be overlooked by those who want to reduce religion to some monolithic thing set in stone. Part of the problem with a good deal of recent atheism is that its conception of God is thoroughly rooted in post-Enlightenment notions of divinity, while it is ignorant of other ways in which the divine has been characterised and conceived. In classical antiquity, for instance, the notion of immanence – that the world existed outside any sort of transcendent realm – would probably to the majority of citizens have been largely incomprehensible.[19] In this connection, Gavin Hyman has written persuasively of the lack of awareness in modern atheism of its cultural specificity, and of the historical matrix out of which it emerged. 'The advent of modernity brought with it a transformed conception of God', Hyman writes, 'a distinctively "modern" theism.' He continues: 'When God is understood to be an object of thought, then God is created in the image of humanity. God comes to be conceived in human terms, his transcendence is domesticated and, in some instances at least, God increasingly takes on the characteristics of a "big person." In effect, God becomes a projection of the human subject'.[20] Dawkins and Hitchens thus see God as a sort of anthropomorphised geriatric sitting up in the clouds, and they very much want to knock him off his cloud-based perch. Yet this image of God as an elevated, floating weirdy beardy is in fact the invention of modernity. It has no relationship to how either classical or medieval people thought about the divine. The medievals, by contrast, saw God as a restless, proactive energy, whose mysterious effects permeated all reality. The Dominican theologian Fergus Kerr helpfully characterises God as being much more like a verb than a noun.[21] This portrait echoes that of another Dominican, Aquinas, for whom God is conceived of not as a personal being who 'exists' but as 'sheer activity, *energeia* – the activity of a triad of action-based relations'.[22]

Furthermore, at the centre of Richard Dawkins' attack on faith and its promulgation is his assumption that religion and science are basically at loggerheads because they constitute rival systems of explaining the world – one of which has veracity and usefulness while the other is useless and harmful. But science and religion are not necessarily even talking about the same things at all. (Why are we here? What happened before the Big Bang? Why are there no apparent limits to the universe? These are not questions to which science can give remotely satisfactory answers.) And if they *are* talking about matters that overlap, or at least are complementary, it is perhaps important that they adopt different registers to do so. As the philosopher and cultural theorist Terry Eagleton perspicuously puts it, 'Dawkins falsely considers that Christianity offers a rival view of the universe to science. He thinks it is a kind of bogus theory or pseudo-explanation of the world. In this sense, he is rather like someone who thinks that a novel is a botched piece of sociology, and who therefore can't see the point of it at all'.[23] This fundamental misapprehension in characterising what religion is actually *for* is further underlined by Christopher Hitchens' brother Peter, who writes (in his elegant riposte to his brother's atheism), that 'those who choose to argue in prose, even if it is very good prose, are unlikely to be receptive to a case which is most effectively couched in poetry'.[24]

Rather than rejecting religion outright – even when what the jihadis and fundamentalists do in the name of religion makes us want to close our eyes in sheer horror – we need to find ways of talking about religion in a manner that does not lead to false dichotomising. It is not true that bad religion is the cause of all the conflicts in the world, or is somehow 'worse' than comparably invidious political or secularist ideologies – as anyone who has cause to reflect on the killing fields of the Khmer Rouge, or the Gulag Archipelago of Alexander Solzhenitsyn, can see only too clearly. Tina Beattie puts it well: 'Contrary to the claims of the New Atheists with their short historical memories, rationalism too has its murdered victims. Have they never heard of the Terror which followed the French Revolution? In 1793, the Goddess of Reason was enthroned in Notre Dame Cathedral in Paris, while her 'devotees' slaughtered tens of thousands during their year-long Reign of Terror, in an outpouring of anti-Christian fervour which particularly victimised Catholic priests'.[25] Indeed, social and cultural fanaticism and ideas other than religious ones have been the root of at least as much pain and suffering in the twentieth century as those of any religious war, and it is simply disingenuous of atheists to pretend otherwise. When the Troubles in Northern Ireland were at their height, much of the conflict centred on governance and power, not on religion, with Catholicism and Protestantism the badges and insignia by which complex questions of identity and belonging were labelled. Religion here was not the cause of conflict but rather one, albeit deeply potent and voluble, vehicle of its expression. It is also the case that the much publicised and widely reported tension in the Middle East between Shia and Sunni Muslims is more often than not about political ambition and ambitious regional power-play than any true or deep-seated animosity bound up with the succession by Ali or Abu Bakr to the Caliphate back in the mid-seventh century. For centuries, across many of the Islamic lands, Shia and Sunni believers lived side by side in relative harmony. It is one of the greatest ironies of ISIS that a grouping committed to restoring the lost lands of 'Islam's golden age' should altogether fail to recognise that the caliphates of the past were frequently characterised as much by their diversity, cosmopolitanism and inclusivism as their hegemony over other faiths. In the 'Abbasid Empire, for example, Jews and Christians were free to worship according to their own religious customs;[26] while in Moorish Spain, Maimonides, a Jew from Cordoba, was celebrated by Muslims as a thinker of brilliance who, in his creative reclamation of Aristotelian thought, had considerable influence on later Islamic science and philosophy.

Whether we profess religious belief or not there needs to be much less certainty or rectitude in matters of religion – whether in professing it, dismissing it or condemning it. Religion has no exclusive claim to rightness, just as atheism has no comparable claim to neutral transparency. Richard Dawkins is a product of the Enlightenment who is defined by a certain set of cultural and intellectual assumptions. As discussed above, his idea of God is itself a limited concept whose meanings and boundaries hardly any ancients or medievals would likely have recognised. They had a different view of the reality around them that was spiritually integrated and holistic. What Dawkins does not seem able to fathom, in absolutising scientific truth, is that there are inevitably limits to scientific and biological rationality. George Steiner is right when he looks to art, music and literature as the best ways of conceptualising something that lies beyond ourselves: the elusive Other that resists definition, restriction or confinement to a set of biological or evolutionary categories. I find myself in full agreement with Steiner when he writes, with a strongly poetic sensibility, that the major forms of human creativity are religious. They enact, he says, 'a root-impulse of the human spirit to explore possibilities of meaning and of truth that lie outside empirical seizure or proof.' He continues: 'So very much in Western art and literature enlists the proposal that we are close neighbours to the unknown, that we move among orders of pragmatic substance themselves permeable to that which lies on the other side, which acts from beyond "the shadow-line"'.[27] It is precisely the question of what lies beyond this elusive 'shadow-line' that ought to animate the truly inquiring mind. Science too is looking for answers. But it has to acknowledge its limitations. Steiner again: 'It is, I believe, poetry, art and music which relate us most directly to that in being which is not ours. Science is no less animate in its making of models and images. But these are not, finally, disinterested. They aim at mastery, at ownership.'[28] It is precisely that sense of exclusivist proprietorialism – whether scientific or religious – which we most urgently need to avoid in attempting to address questions of meaning, truth and ultimacy while avoiding a facile reductionism.

It is an openness and receptiveness to possibility that enables us – not always, but sometimes, in the right mood and place and light – to catch a glimpse of something else: that mysterious something which lies beyond the register of what we can see or know. It was not through any conviction that God was demonstratively 'there' which sent a formerly disbelieving Peter Hitchens back to church – rather the sense that, within the resonating stonework of a distinctively English cathedral, and in the liturgy and music of its Evensong, there might be something happening which was elusive but nevertheless important: 'This sunset ceremony is the very heart of English Christianity', Hitchens writes. 'The prehistoric, mysterious poetry of the Magnificat and the Nunc Dimittis, perhaps a melancholy evening hymn, and the cold, ancient lament and curses of the Psalms, as the unique slow dusk of England gathers outside and inside the echoing, haunted, impossibly old building, are extraordinarily potent. If you welcome them, they have an astonishing power to reassure and comfort. If you suspect or mistrust them, they will alarm and repel you like a strong and unwanted magic, something to flee from before it takes hold.'[29] While the liturgy can indeed draw you in if you approach it in the right spirit, it can also push you away if you start to reflect on the tensions between its antique and improbable mythologising and a current worldview dominated by Post-Enlightenment rationalism. But such uncertainty about the veracity of what we see and hear is in a way the whole point of religion. We are invited to believe precisely because we cannot know.

Life is not a set of propositions to be understood but a series of mysterious questions in the light of whose ambiguities and ambivalences we find ourselves continually reshaped. I want to make a pragmatic if not philosophical case in favour of agnosticism: for recognition of the practical value of mystery and that sometimes a confession of uncertainty is as valuable to us as a profession of faith. The following chapter will explore this idea in more depth. But in recognising atheism as still a minority position in the West (Grace Davie, Linda Woodhead and others have shown that many people still retain a residual sense of commitment to belief, but without expressing it in the public way that was once common), we also have to guard against the idea that human thinking leads us on a straight course to divine truth. When I moved to north Norfolk with my former wife I was certain that our life together would begin and end in that part of the country, and that our partnership was solid and certain. I could not envisage any other reality. Yet our marriage foundered and all certainties exploded into dust. At the time this felt like the end of everything real. Divorce had an immense impact not just on my emotional and psychological wellbeing but on that of my wider family as well. The ramifications of losing wife, home and certainty are still reverberating and their aftershocks may be with me always. But in remarrying, relocating and generally recalibrating my life I have experienced a richness of difference and unexpectedness that have led me down pathways and avenues that I could never then have imagined. I still miss intensely the landscapes of the coast and the intimacy of a relationship that still exists, but always in a different time: inaccessible except through memory. However, in the crucible of the unknown I have been, I think, interestingly redefined: more open-minded, possibly; less willing to accept second best, quite probably; and above all, better prepared to explore the hinterlands of difference, even when the roads through the marshes may be obscured by

[handwritten margin note: false certainty]

29

fog. So how we are shaped and defined may be as much by what we aren't, and don't possess, than by what we are – or think we are – and currently have to hand. That seems to me to be just as true of religious belief. In talking about God we are by definition talking about something unfathomable, unknowable – something ungraspable, except obliquely through the language of poetry and metaphor. The medieval mystics understood this better than anyone. That is why they talked in enigmatic terms about opposites: about absence and negativity and darkness. They knew very well that at best human beings may catch only a furtive glimpse of the invisible, may hear a barely audible whisper of the unsayable: and that divine presence is actually only 'present' through the faint shadow it casts on the grass as your blinded eyes look into the sun.

Out at Thornham Eye, where the river Glaven empties into the North Sea, there used to stand a chapel where a priest from the nearby Carmelite Friary at Blakeney would bless ships setting out on their voyages to the Baltic and Icelandic sea lanes and then collect grateful tributes on the mariners' return.[30] Apart from a jumble of stones the chapel is long gone, but the handsome gabled archway visible on the coastal road in Cley-next-the-Sea is said to be a remnant of that holy building. At Wiveton, just across the former tidal Glaven estuary from Cley, a fourteenth-century bridge straddles the now unassuming river. If you look down, and look hard enough, you can see close to the waterline a modest portal cut into the stonework. It is thought that here, for many centuries, was placed an image or likeness of the Virgin, perhaps beside a candle, to which the sailors of 100-ton ships, now ocean-bound from inland Glandford, would direct nervous entreaties for a safe seaborne return.[31] This landscape is a sacred one. Its times and tides were counterpointed by the complementary rhythms of a thriving maritime trade and earnest religious devotion. Though the image of the Virgin is lost, and the friars' chapel vanished, the contours of this remarkable region's spirituality are everywhere discernible – if you seek for them determinedly. There is richness and gain to be had from hiddenness: from having to look hard enough for things concealed just above or below the waterline: that are not visible at first glance. The same is true of the unlikely marram grass or saxifrage that can be seen on top of the windswept dune at Holkham Bay: in all that immensity of sand and violent, pounding empty space there is an abundance of life and vegetation. To find it, you have only to know where to seek for it.

Perhaps one of the reasons why it is so hard in the twenty-first century to talk with credibility about the notion of 'God' is that many people have lost sight of how to refer to the divine analogically, with meaningful – and therefore truthful – reference to symbol, metaphor and creative approximation. Gavin Hyman notes that 'For Aquinas, the fundamental problem with theological language is that language in general has been developed by creatures to refer to creaturely things. It is therefore inadequate – and potentially misleading – when applied to God'.[32] Aquinas therefore resorted to analogy in order to try to conceptualise the divine, and not cut ourselves off from God altogether. Once an analogical understanding of language is lost, Hyman notes, theology has no defence against the charge (made by Marx and Feuerbach, for example) that God is no more than a human 'projection'. The result is a God whose transcendence is domesticated, conceived in increasingly worldly or anthropomorphised terms. If he becomes too obviously a 'big person', the notion of the divine becomes increasingly superfluous and empty – and all too open to atheistic attack. The Church Fathers had no such difficulty in speaking analogically. Clement of Alexandria and Anselm treat the seven days of creation as allegory and not as history. Athanasius speaks of paradise as a 'figure'. What was important to them was the spiritual teaching, not historical fact. Furthermore, the medieval world held to a conception of time wherein there were different 'orders' of time corresponding to secular, sacred and other dimensions of being. The medievals had no difficulty, in fact, in conceptualising truth as poetical and metaphorical, not as literal. In our fact-, time- and gadget-obsessed modern world, we have lost something precious and profound: the capacity to hit the right note in regard to the transcendent – one that is not profoundly tone-deaf. The early medieval mind was not deficient or lacking because it had no access to a telescope. It was by no means contemptible because it saw the stars as tiny rends in the fabric of the sky, through which the white light of heaven glimmeringly shone through. In such an image it was rather saying something important and true about what lies beyond the human capacity to grasp the unfathomable – in scientific terms, about the very limits of the universe.

The lonely dune, the vacant portal in the bridge: but a loneliness leavened by wildflowers and an emptiness resonant with history and the echo of heartfelt devotion. Rowan Williams has written of finding meaning, following the terrorist attack on the Twin Towers of New York City, in the suffocating dust of Ground Zero.[33] Even writing in the dust can result in words that scorch one's heart. God must be sought in the shadows as well as in the sunlight; in those yawning and aching spaces of emptiness that sometimes threaten to swallow us up whole – in abandonment, in depression, in the misery felt by those who are left behind. It is here, in the very midst of the black waters, that we can learn especially from those mystics of the Middle Ages who turned to images and metaphors not of light (as one might have expected them to, since light is so often associated with the divine), but of darkness. Using apophatic language (describing not what God is, but what he is not), the author of the *Cloud of Unknowing* speaks of a divinity 'hidden' from experience. Light is darkness, knowing is unknowing – a cloud – and the pain of contemplating it is the agony of contemplating more reality that can actually be borne: 'man may not see me and live'.[34] Gregory of Nyssa writes in strikingly comparable terms about a tantalising not-seeing seeing obscured by a cloud: 'It is precisely in this that true knowledge of what is sought consists, and precisely in this that seeing consists, that is in not seeing, because we seek what lies beyond all knowledge, shrouded by incomprehensibility in all directions, as it were by some cloud'.[35] Similarly, Simone Weil writes in this hauntingly elusive but nevertheless compelling way about divine activity manifested paradoxically and vitally in absence: 'Contact with human creatures is given us through the sense of presence. Contact with God is given us through the sense of absence. Compared with this absence, presence becomes more absent than absence.'[36] My own experience of depression, following the misery of losing a wife whom I loved, suggests that any conception of God as light would have been wholly misplaced. If there were any deity that made sense it would have to be a deity that truly understood what abandonment meant. This would be a God who knew what it meant to lose everything that you held to be of value. It would hunker down with you in the dark pit, and it would sit with you there at the bottom as water trickled down from a distant patch of sky above you, impossibly far away and impossible to reach.

Ambiguity, not certainty, is redolent with both mystery and promise. The Norfolk coast that I loved during my first marriage, and is associated with my ex-wife and with home, is lost to me. It can never come again, at least in the form in which it existed then: bound up with agonising associations to do with my life with her. And yet, in purely physical form, it endures. Like the Church of St Nicholas at Salthouse it is still there – rain and storm-battered, maybe, but stolidly present. This shore is a graveyard of ships, but not of hopes, even of dreams. One can return to it, to seek the flower in the hidden crevice. Out there, on the endless sands, it may be there is something lying: something waiting for us which at the moment we cannot see. So let us return to analogy, to the language of poetry. In her beautifully realised medieval novel *The Leper's Companions*, a relatively undiscovered masterpiece of British magic realism, Julia Blackburn brings us face to face with the impossible other:

> 'The man was poised in indecision, staring at the thing which lay heaped at his feet. I saw then that it was not a human corpse, or the trunk of a tree, or a bundle of sail that he had found, but a mermaid. She was lying facedown, her body twisted into a loose curl, her hair matted with scraps of seaweed.
>
> The year was fourteen hundred and ten, and it was very early in the morning, with the sun pushing its way gently through a covering of mist that floated aimlessly over the land and the water.
>
> The man had never seen a mermaid before except for the one carved in stone above the east door of the church. She had very pointed teeth and a double tail like two soft and tapering legs, while this one had a single tail which could have belonged to a large halibut or a cod.
>
> The man stepped forward and squatted down beside her. The pattern of her interlinking scales glinted with an oily light. He stroked them along the direction in which they lay and they were wet and slippery, leaving a coat of slime on his palm. But when his hand moved over the pale skin off her back it was dry and cold and as rough as a cat's tongue.
>
> He lifted a hank of dark hair, feeling its weight. Little translucent shrimps were tangled within its mesh and struggling to free themselves. A yellow crab scuttled around the curve of the waist and dropped out of sight.
>
> He hesitated for a moment, but then he took hold of the mermaid's shoulders and rolled her over. The sand clung

in patches on her body like the map of some forgotten country. Her nipples were red as sea anemones. Her navel was deep and round. Her eyes were wide open and as blue as the sky could ever be. As he gazed at her, a lopsided smile drifted over her face.'[37]

Mermaids they may not be, but regarded from a distance common and grey seals can look very much like human beings, while on the sands and strandline of Holkham the sea is forever discharging objects that bring us face to face with the past and with enigma. I have seen up close a solitary grey seal pup washed up by the ebb tide which, like Blackburn's mermaid, looked mighty pleased with itself as it lay there basking in the sun. Holkham Bay is an indeterminate and liminal terrain, full of wonders – much like the landscape of belief. It may be true that in the contemporary West we have lost sight of religious orthodoxies. It may well be the case that churchgoing is in terminal decline. But neither is atheism a popular answer.[38] Perhaps the twilight world of ambiguity – of openness to the unexpected, and to the language of mystery – is a much less uncomfortable place to be than many assume. The Trappist monk and twentieth-century mystic Thomas Merton once famously said that 'We believe, not because we want to *know*, but because we want to *be*.' It is within the landscapes of longing that we experience precisely that sense of connectedness with our truest selves, with the selves that lie buried within, even at the bottom of the pit of misery. These are the selves that can best articulate mystery through creativity and imagination, through simile and metaphor and poetic device. We may see no mermaids on Holkham beach, but a persisting belief in the supernatural deeps has over the centuries shaped the folklore of the coast and its enduring narrative culture. Those beliefs have long memories and they have staying power. They are amplifiers which enable us to get in touch with that sense of the transcendent which potentially, if only we could hear it, lies at the heart of all of us – whether in music, appreciation of art, or opera, or an exquisite wineglass pulpit in the peaceful Norfolk church of Burnham Norton.[39] Another great Christian thinker, Augustine, considered God to be 'everywhere but not everywhere to us. There is but one point in the Universe where God communicates with us, and that is the centre of our own soul.'[40] In all our current debates about religion, in all the fierce business of indignant protest and affirmation, there is surely room for recognition that the suggestive and haunting landscapes of ambiguity may have more to tell us about both ourselves and the divine than any passionately certain denunciation either of God or of godlessness.

Chapter Two

DOUBT

'Take care that you do not believe that you can understand the incomprehensible.'

– Bonaventure

'The whole problem with the world is that fools and fanatics are always so certain of themselves, and wiser people so full of doubts.'

– Bertrand Russell

We are holding hands on a visit to neighbouring Suffolk: connected by flesh yet separated by virtually everything else. Her touch feels elusive, withheld – like her essence. Later, over lunch, my mother chats with us brightly. For her, this is a meeting like any other. The woman at my side, seemingly so familiar but now so very far away, nods distractedly in agreement. Her eyes, a startling lapis, hold my mother's gaze; but her expression is neutral, cool: distant. Plans are made; calendars and future trips discussed. On the surface all is well. Underneath, deep water currents are raging and gathering as the floodgates of our shared life, now assaulted by the colossal mass of *untold lakes of feeling, begin to split asunder. Later, at home, my wife turns to look at me: 'I miss you', I say. 'I know', is her reply. So it begins, that terrible paradox: the termination of a union alongside anticipation of the bitter miseries ahead. Endings and beginnings: the beginning of the end. The cloud descends, implacably – as blinding and stifling and disorienting as an unavoidable spray of mustard gas. It is the cloud of unknowing, of forgetting. Already I can see our past begin to dissolve: soon, it will shrivel to nothing.*

Let us travel backwards now: away from the life that is unravelling to a future that's unfolding. Five years earlier my fiancée and I face each other the evening before our wedding. Dinner is complete. The guests are due tomorrow. The preparations, a year in the making, are done. 'Are you ready?' I ask. 'As ready as I'll ever be' she replies. The talking is over. It is time for both of us to decide: and the fates are gathering, seating themselves for our ceremony in the Elizabethan hall below. The morning after, my hands do not seem to function as they should. I am trembling: made clumsy by anxiety I can neither tie shoelaces nor button up my shirt. Panicking, I phone a friend, clinging to the raft of past attachment like a castaway hauling himself to safety from the ocean. 'Am I doing the right thing?' I ask. My friend hesitates; her silence is profound. An eternity of feeling passes between us in a moment. 'Of course', she replies. It is the only answer she can give. But neither of us is convinced.

Bunched in clusters of wreck and decay, razor shells, clamshells and periwinkles are scattered behind us like so many broken bones. And below the swell, whispering like the merfolk whose glistening tails thrash beneath our ships, lie Norfolk's vanished forests and primordial hunting grounds. Under the relentless waves is a world that came and went, that time after time lived and laughed as we did: all the men and women and their children who traversed the great tundra plain, stretching away under the North Sea: washed away. All that remains is their soughing, melancholy after-breath. Think not so ill of me, in those granite hills where now you walk, or beside those shores whose waves I will never see or hear with you again, that you cannot remember us as once we were. Think rather of the flocks of seabirds that we watched together from Holkham beach: the oystercatchers, redshank and curlew whose piping, mournful calls were all too prescient. Think of the winding, mysterious creeks, those secret places where you and I would walk together in the steaming mudflats. An underworld opened out to us there, beckoning and calling siren-voiced; in we fell, stuck fast like ragworm and lugworm beached on a coastal reedbed. Just as now I am stranded in a far deeper abyss of yearning.

Why should the highways and byways of our lives be clearly laid out? Why should our routes and stories be maps that are straightforward to read and decipher? Similarly, why should the boundaries between faith and unbelief be instantly recognisable? The landscapes of longing are not so easily charted or defined. The stumps of trees visible at low tide in Brancaster Bay, known as 'sleepers' by generations of Norfolk men and women, eloquently speak of a sunken world of woods and forests that once extended as far as Norway. Fishing boats still periodically return from the North Sea with an improbable catch: the tusk of a mammoth, trawled from the bottom of a seabed that once teemed with Neolithic wildlife. This is a landscape criss-crossed by hidden pathways: a palimpsest of lives and loves now lost and overlaid by the corresponding preoccupations of the individuals and peoples who followed in their ancestors' wake. The Peddars Way, one of the ancient tracks which run across the verdant Norfolk countryside, in all likelihood did not reach its final terminus at coastal Holme-next-the-Sea: most probably there was a ferry crossing there which the Roman legions used for fast transportation of soldiers and goods from nearby Lincolnshire, at a point on the adjacent coast quite near Skegness, to their territories in East Anglia and beyond. When, faced with increasing and threatening Anglo-Saxon incursions and piracy, the Emperor Honorius withdrew his troops from Britain in 410 AD, this antique Roman crossing across the Wash – just like the drowned tundra plain beneath the smothering waves of the German Ocean – passed into memory and folklore.

Perhaps it is this sense of a landscape concealed beneath, or sometimes alongside, the topography that is visible today which so attracted my former wife and me to settle in a region whose past has always been more than usually rich and resonant. It was here, for example, that the Vikings came ashore in the late ninth century, first for plunder and then for a place to call home. Several settlements that end in the Danish suffix 'by' (meaning a village or homestead) are clustered near to Yarmouth. Meanwhile, Calthorpe and Saxthorpe – northwest of the town of Aylsham – betray their own Scandinavian heritage in their different endings: the word 'thorpe' signified a farm. And a Viking footfall can be heard too at Brancaster Staithe and at Burnham Overy Staithe, both popular now with walkers and sailors: 'stoth' is the Old Norse noun for landing stage. While Suffolk has a mere five settlements that can be traced to incursions by the Viking armies and the farmers who followed, Norfolk has as many as two dozen. This cussed maritime county, which has always faced eastwards, towards the Low Countries and Scandinavia, was on the very frontline of invasion and migration. Borderlands are invariably locations where interesting things take place; and it was in these liminal regions that different peoples professing competing faiths first rubbed up alongside one another – to begin with in conflict (resulting in destruction by the Great Heathen Army of the Anglo-Saxon kingdom of East Anglia and martyrdom of King Edmund, England's first patron saint, in 869) and then in attempts at mutual understanding, barter and commerce. In the end, perhaps after many misunderstandings and much difficulty, these communities mingled and joined together, there was inter-marriage, paganism gave way (though perhaps not so quickly as some might like to think) to Christianity, and Thor, Loki, Odin and Freya eventually took second place to the more enduring myth of the God who became man in first century Palestine and died to rise again on the third day.

One of the themes of this book is that the provisional and the uncertain have not been peripheral but actually vital to the process of belief: and that conviction offers no safe or ultimately satisfactory route to understanding the divine. The things buried beneath layers of Norfolk chalk, clay and history – that sense of the mysterious: of matters concealed, forgotten or not immediately discernible – become a helpful metaphor for precisely the idea that we need to look deeper and adopt a wider perspective if we wish to garner a better sense of the universe and what it might mean. Faith is never an easy road. Nor should it be. The fact of exile from a place long-loved, or the irrevocable loss of a lover or spouse with whom one wished over many years to build a life – these, while crushing to the soul, can also serve to heighten one's appreciation of the things that can never come again but without whose loss we could never be truly human. The unfairly neglected English novelist John Cowper Powys wrote some of his most deeply personal, reflective Wessex novels from across the Atlantic, while working as a jobbing lecturer in America. Perhaps the extraordinary, concentrated lyricism of books like *Wolf Solent*, *Weymouth Sands* and (his masterpiece) *A Glastonbury Romance*, would have been impossible to realise if they had taken shape within the very landscapes they describe. It was the fact of distance, separation – of a melancholy, deeply felt ennui – which enabled his imagination to take full flight. Removed now from the landscapes in Norfolk that I love, I cannot experience them sensorially, in the present, but I can see them keenly in my mind's eye. I cannot touch daily the magnificent octagonal stone font of St Margaret's of Antioch in Cley-next-the-Sea; I cannot taste the briny evening air above Kelling Heath, following a sudden rain shower, which makes each hanging leaf shine like glass; I cannot hear the crunch of pebbles and sand beneath my feet as I embrace and celebrate the enormity of sky on Salthouse beach – but I can imagine those things in a way that summons, through my sense of continuing loss and longing, their bright, brilliant and intrinsic essence. Removal from these landscapes paradoxically helps me to find a way into their mystery, of what they really signify.

The idea of hiddenness, at least as it relates to faith, perhaps finds its most intriguing form of expression in the lives and works of some of the medieval mystics. The very word 'mystic' is derived from the Greek word *mystikos*, which means 'hidden' or 'obscure'. So any discussion of religious concealment will likely benefit from engagement with the writings of those Christian solitaries, anchorites and visionaries who grappled with the paradox of expressing a faith based on the invisible and infinite. Moreover, it is perhaps no accident that Norfolk in the Middle Ages produced a cluster of individuals whose actions and writings represent some of the most remarkable expressions of inspired religiosity in the history of Christian mystical contemplation. Norfolk was at one time one of England's most populous areas, and before the horrifying calamity of the Black Death Norwich was second only to London in size and prosperity. The religious life of the region was correspondingly diverse and colourful, taking on a robust counter-cultural complexion – sometimes culminating in outright stubbornness – for which Norfolk people are still notorious. Eamon Duffy has argued that East Anglia, commanded to fall into line with Reformation practice and a new Prayer Book, relinquished its Catholic liturgies, feast-days and saints only reluctantly and at best half-heartedly.[1] Robert Kett's rebellion in 1549, while predominantly a violent reaction against yeoman land enclosures, also it appears had a strong religious undertow.[2] A century earlier, the heresy of Lollardy was notably popular here. And it was in this context – surrounded by a landscape that has always been defined by the sea: where seascape and landscape combine to form a hybrid that is itself atavistic and mystical – that three women came to prominence in forging a number of different but closely interlinked manifestations of Christianity that were as distinctive as the place they inhabited.

If you travel to the village of Little Walsingham today there is little on the surface to suggest that, like its neighbour Bury St Edmunds across the Suffolk border, it was once one of the greatest shrines in Europe. From the 1930s onwards the town revived as a pilgrimage centre to the degree that it now attracts 250,000 visitors yearly. But before the Dissolution of the Monasteries this was England's Mecca – somewhere that every Englishman felt compelled to visit at least once during his lifetime. Walsingham is now a quiet place of picturesque, half-timbered medieval buildings. Should you visit on a weekday, it often feels as if you can have the place almost to yourself. Through a gap in the large and imposing oak door on the High Street you can catch a glimpse – standing on a wide and verdant lawn surrounded by snowdrops and daffodils in spring, and cornflowers and cow-parsley in summer – of the remains of the twelfth-century Augustinian Priory, whose large East Window is the sole structure of substance still upright. It seems an unlikely place for magic realism. Yet it was precisely here that a widow of Norman origin, Richelde or Richeldis de Faverches,[3] whose family most probably came from Fervaques in the modern *département* of Calvados, around 1130 (the year of her widowhood)[4] had three astonishing visions in which the Virgin Mary instructed her to build a replica of the Holy House of Nazareth in Walsingham Parva (the original Anglo-Saxon settlement and now the site of the parish church). Despite her devotion to the Virgin, Richard Pynson's *Ballad*[5] – written perhaps as early as 1465 – suggests that Richeldis was overcome with doubt and astonishment. 'She again travelled with Our Lady to Nazareth', writes Nicole Marzac-Holland, 'where the self-same injunction was given her.' Noting the measurements and arrangements of the house, doubts still assailed her: 'Was the vision real? Would she know how to build the house?'.[6] Through divine guidance and agency the Holy House finally took shape by the banks of the winding River Stiffkey, and not long afterwards the Priory was founded alongside it. Thus began the Walsingham shrine.

Self-doubt features too in the story of Norfolk's – and perhaps England's – greatest mystical writer of the Middle Ages. In the mid-fourteenth century, a time of war, uncertainty and general social upheaval, when the Black Death had bled her city white and two-thirds of its clergy were dead, Julian of Norwich (later an anchorite in St Julian's Church in King Street) experienced fifteen 'showings' or revelations where she was permitted to see and understand the mysteries of Christ's Passion. The *Revelations of Divine Love*, in both their long and short versions, are harrowing and chilling in their visceral depiction of pain and suffering, and as one commentator has said 'utterly appropriate to our own blood-soaked age'.[7] Yet for all the intensity of her experience of God and Christ, Julian too experienced uncertainty. As her revelations ceased, Julian's head ached beyond belief and she was assailed by doubts: she allowed logic to convince her that her own imagination might have tricked her into these visions. Assailed by the devil, she felt she was being strangled. It seemed that her house was on fire 'and she retched at the stench'. The culmination of her story in the famous but enigmatic assurance that 'all shall be well, and all manner of things shall be well' does not suggest that the panic and uncertainty instilled in her by her vocation was of little or no consequence. At one point Julian feels driven towards insanity. And looking back on her life, after forty years of devotion to God – a recluse from the world between the unchanging four walls of her cell – she asks 'Why ... why? Why Lord?'[8]

Norfolk's third mystical presence, the irrepressibly loquacious but nevertheless likeable Margery Kempe, was a native of King's – then Bishop's – Lynn. Margery, who met and talked with Julian in Norwich, experienced her own sense of strong incertitude. Born in 1373 (the year Julian received her showings), Margery's is the first biography to have come down to us in English. It is a picaresque rollercoaster of a ride, which conducts the reader breathlessly down the highways and byways not just of East Anglia or England but of the whole medieval Mediterranean. From Lynn to Venice and from Venice to Jaffa, Jerusalem and Santiago it is nevertheless a story solidly rooted in the author's homeland and sense of definite locality. As Marzac-Holland rightly says, 'the author paints a vivid picture of life in Norfolk in the fifteenth century: the town and the country; the rich and the poor; the merchants, churchmen and sailors. Her book is peppered with Norfolk humour and poetic descriptions of landscapes. She knew the great of the land; she conversed with them, argued with them, was imprisoned by them, fêted by them'.[9] The particular affliction, or gift, of Margery Kempe was to burst into 'boisterous sobbing and plenteous weeping' whenever she considered the fact of Christ's Passion or heard a homily on the topic. Such was the social opprobrium (many people thought 'she could weep and desist as she liked'), and the unpopularity and misfortune that resulted (including robbery of her possessions on board ship to the Holy Land, and several dangerous accusations of Lollardy), that she wished her shameful gift to be removed. But Christ made it clear to her that 'it was her own way of salvation and she must abide by it'.[10] The desire of Margery Kempe to attain closer union with the man of sorrows necessitated a difficult and challenging voyage: not just an actual journey away from her familiar Norfolk to witness the physical places of Christ's suffering in Palestine, or a journey into poverty and near-destitution on the streets of medieval Rome, but also a psychological trip into embarrassment, self-mortification and ridicule. In the early days of my separation from my ex-wife, which then turned into months, I too felt the acute embarrassment and social stigma of a deeply unwanted gift. All the security and familiarity which accompanied being part of an accepted couple – of being married – was gone. And yet the disorienting wanderings which resulted were, just like Margery's, surprising and transformative.

These three Norfolk mystics – Richelde, Julian and Margery Kempe – demonstrate in their devotion to God and Christ that unbelief was not an option. Their various mystical visions are full of varied and colourful professions of faith and a desire for better knowledge of and intimacy with the divine. Yet the ways they believed show plenty of room for irresolution, hesitancy and doubt. Richelde initially suspected the veracity of her vision. Julian thought she was being led astray by the devil. Margery wanted rid of her socially excluding outbursts, whether divinely inspired or not. These remarkable and fascinating women demonstrate to us, in ways that are distinctively rooted in the Norfolk soil they called home, that faith is not a straightforward path. It is as twisting, winding and uncertain a road as any route taken by Margery Kempe to the Holy Land. But with perseverance, and a combination of tenacity, resolution and courage, one might end up somewhere worth getting to.

Wider consideration of medieval mysticism reveals similar ambiguities and ambivalences. These mystics never doubt the fact of God's reality, and would have had little or no understanding of the post-Enlightenment, rationalistic conception of God as a transcendent entity on a cloud dictating human affairs from his heavenly empyrean. They certainly would not have understood Dawkins' atheism. They do however face persistent questions to do with a sense of God's absence – not of his absolute non-existence but of his utter removal from their sense and perception of him. Anselm, the Abbot of Bec in Normandy who succeeded Lanfranc to the See of Canterbury in 1093, did not – despite his elevation to the top job in the English church – always feel close to God. For example, in this heartfelt passage he writes: 'Oh supreme and unapproachable light, oh holy and blessed truth, how far art Thou from me who am so near to Thee, how far art Thou removed from my vision, though I am so near to Thine! Everywhere Thou art wholly present, and I see Thee not. In Thee I move and in Thee I have my being, and cannot come to Thee; Thou art within me and about me, and I feel Thee not'.[11] Elsewhere in his enigmatic, sinewy and often elusive philosophical writings Anselm elaborates on the idea of the immensity of God and the limitations of human beings in finding him and experiencing his presence:

> *'If I have not found my God*
> > *what is it that I have found and understood*
> > *so truly and certainly?*
>
> *But if I have found him,*
> > *why do I not experience what I have found?*
>
> *Lord God,*
> > *if my soul has found you,*
> > *why has it no experience of you?'*[12]

Nowadays we tend to think of mysticism – or the generic term 'spirituality' which is often used almost synonymously with medieval mystical phenomena and writing – as wholly bound up with some kind of transformation of the self. We think of mysticism as an activity or process of contemplation that will transform our inner, spiritual lives so that our experience of the divine will be transformed somehow for the better. (Given the emphasis on the individual in modern life, it comes as no great surprise that spirituality too should have taken a somewhat introverted turn.) By this reckoning, mysticism becomes almost as much about the self as it is about God. It is thus fundamentally *experiential*. But this is really a misreading of the medieval mystical intent, especially as it found expression in England (one of the most fertile and singular theatres for mystical activity in medieval Europe). Denys Turner writes about this as follows: 'Whereas our employment of the metaphors of "inwardness" and "ascent" appears to be tied in with the achievement and the cultivation of a certain kind of experience – such as those recommended within the practice of what is called, nowadays, "centring" or "contemplative" prayer – the mediaeval employment of them was tied in with a "critique" of such religious experiences and practices. Whereas we appear to have "psychologised" the metaphors, the Neoplatonic mediaeval writer used the metaphors in an "apophatic" spirit to play down the value of the "experiential"; and that, therefore, whereas it would come naturally to the contemporary, "psychologising" mind to think of "the mystical" in terms of its characterising *experiences*, the mediaeval mind thought of the "mystical", that is to say, the "hidden" or "secret", wisdom as being what the Author of *The Cloud of Unknowing* called a "divinity" which is "hidden" precisely from experience'.[13] In other words, many of the medieval mystics – especially the author of *The Cloud of Unknowing*, to whom we shall come in a moment – were focused not on accentuating the experience of the self in order to make the self somehow 'better' or more 'spiritual', but were trying rather to map a route to finding or understanding God through use predominantly of a language not of what God is but of what he isn't.

The medievals, though they would not perhaps have put it in those terms, realised absolutely the dangers of self-absorption and self-orientation: that God was not a mere object of human attention as much as the absolute subject worthy of that consideration. It is because he is both the beginning and the end of the cosmos, alpha and omega, as well as utterly beyond it, that mystical speaking of God is, as Bernard McGinn puts it, 'a strategy for saying the unsayable'.[14] It is for this reason that so many mystics 'have wrestled with the paradox that God is found in absence and negation more than in presence'.[15] Their profound, difficult and sometimes seemingly self-contradictory apophaticism is exemplified, for example, by Nicholas of Cusa (who drew on the writings of the Dominican mystical thinker Meister Eckhart), in his treatise *On the Vision of God*. Here we find the idea that seeing God is invariably a paradoxical 'not-seeing seeing'. As McGinn explains, 'God', according to this interpretation, 'is never the object of seeing but is always its subject'.[16] Or, as Meister Eckhart expressed it in this famous statement: 'The eye in which I see God is the same eye in which God sees me'.[17]

One of the most mysterious and compelling attempts in Christian literature to speak in plausible terms about the infinite – to articulate an intelligible sense of what God might be in terms of what he isn't – can be found in the words of *The Cloud of Unknowing*. This anonymous English mystical text, written in the second half of the fourteenth century, famously speaks of a cloud or 'darkness' of unknowing that lies between his readers and knowledge of God. The *Cloud* author writes: 'If you wish to enter into this cloud, to be at home in it, and to take up the contemplative work of love as I urge you to, there is something else you must do. Just as the *cloud of unknowing* lies above you, between you and your God, so you must fashion a *cloud of forgetting* beneath you, between you and every created thing. The *cloud of unknowing* will perhaps leave you with the feeling that you are far from God. But no, if it is authentic, only the absence of a *cloud of forgetting* keeps you from him now'.[18] The cloud of unknowing is here the darkness of ignorance that lies between human beings and a God who is concealed and far away from them; whereas the cloud of forgetting appears to be a focused condition of contemplation of an absolute reality that distances the person both from the self and from every earthly distraction. This remarkably evocative and powerful language is interesting above all for its emphasis on the fact that God can be hard to reach.

The idea that mystical reflection is challenging and demanding finds resonance in the writings of many others. St John of the Cross, for example, speaks of a dark contemplation that is painful to the soul: 'But it may be asked: Why does the soul call the divine light that enlightens the soul and purges it of its ignorances a dark night? The answer to this is that for two reasons this divine wisdom is not only night and darkness, but also pain and torment. The first is because the divine wisdom is so high that it transcends the capacity of the soul, and therefore in that respect is darkness. The second reason is based on the meanness and impurity of the soul, and in that respect the divine wisdom is painful to it, afflictive, and also dark'.[19] Several other medieval mystics have written in broadly comparable terms of the trials and trauma of mystical purification: that it often involves extreme suffering and also, and all too often, personal dereliction. Though their faith in the power and reality of God is a touchstone which recurs, God can still be a harsh and unyielding taskmaster. Often he absents himself completely, leading to accusations of capriciousness and bad behaviour from his acolytes. Teresa of Avila once said to God: 'Lord, if this is the way you treat your friends, no wonder you have so few of them'.[20] In similar vein, the troubled Umbrian mystic Angela of Foligno (*c.* 1250–1309), a member of the women's third order of Franciscans, felt tormented by demons, to the degree that she perceived there to be no supernatural support for her soul. She writes (in *The Memorial*), in a language painfully resonant with fear, as well as resentment towards God, of times of doubt and suffering: 'There are times when I cry without being able to stop. There are times when such great anger ensues that I am scarcely able to stop without tearing myself apart. There are also times when I can't hold myself back from striking myself in a horrible way, and sometimes my head and limbs are swollen. When the soul begins to see all the virtues fall down and fall away, then there is fear and lament, and I speak to God, calling out again and again to God without let up, saying to him, "My Son, my Son, do not leave me, my Son!".[21] And the medieval Beguine mystic Hadewijch speaks tantalisingly of something called 'unfaith' – a loving doubt in relation to God which deepens the soul: 'Unfaith (*ontrouwe*) made them [those in pursuit of God] so deep that they wholly engulfed *minne* [God as love] and dared to fight her with sweet and bitter' (*Vision* 13).[22]

If many mystics have at times felt abandoned by God, it is perhaps in the form of the Dominican philosopher and thinker Meister Eckhart (*c.* 1260 – *c.* 1328) that this sense of abandonment[23] reaches its theological apex. Accused of heresy in 1326, and posthumously censured by the papal authorities in 1329, Eckhart was an unsettling figure whose unorthodox language, intended to appeal to a lay as well as clerical audience, was perhaps bound to come under unfavourable scrutiny during the difficult years of the Papacy's 'Babylonian Exile' in Avignon. In his sermon on the 'poverty of spirit', Eckhart writes cryptically: 'I ask God that he rid me of God'. Some scholars, including John Caputo, have referred to this idea as a kind of 'mystical atheism'.[24] It is an attempt, as Caputo sees it, to conceptualise the absolute nothingness and the abyss of God's being 'and the utter impotence of any metaphysical theology to seize Him with its concepts.'[25] Such a desire on Eckhart's part to be rid of the manifest God in order to be open to the hidden God (what Eckhart calls the '*Gottheit* in *Gott*', or 'Godhead within God'[26]) was, as Caputo has suggested, 'profoundly shocking to the churchmen of his day.'[27] Yet far from being a rejection of his Dominican background, and the scholasticism of his order's founder, Aquinas, this creative pushing by Eckhart at the boundaries of what God is and is not was arguably an extension and radicalisation of Thomist scholasticism, not – as his detractors thought – a denial of it. However, an enigmatic opacity about God was in this instance far too potent a brew to be tolerable. Ambiguity invariably has a difficult relationship with orthodoxy in times of trouble, when often it has been seen as a threat rather than an opportunity for deepening religiosity.

Modern atheism it may not be; but doubt and even at times a kind of proto-agnosticism there is here a-plenty. Even so whistle-stop a tour as this one, of sparingly selected medieval mystical writings, reveals a trope that crops up time and again: that God is concealed, is often perplexingly *in absentia*, and is revealed as much by what we cannot say about him as what we can. This is hardly a recipe for blind certainty about faith or of the easy relationship of human beings to the divine. That God is love is an undoubted anchor of mystical assumption in the Middle Ages. Outright unbelief is not a viable option for the mystics, nor would it have made much sense within a worldview where God was as much immanent as transcendent. But within this basic framework of an affirmation of divinity, there is considerable scope nonetheless for a sense of irresolution, resentment and even of abandonment. God, for the devoted medieval, is not always an anchor or a rock in the storm. What becomes clear, in any portrayal of how the medieval mystics related to the idea of the divine, is that it was precisely uncertainty about access to its presence that so often gave rise to their most profound insights into the joys of mystical union.

Perhaps, in the light of this, it should come as no great surprise that when 'mystical theology' (as distinct from mysticism or mystical contemplation) developed as a distinctive discipline in the seventeenth century, especially in commentaries that clustered round the Carmelites Teresa of Avila and John of the Cross, many loose, expansive and beautifully ambiguous medieval mystical ideas were harmonised as much as possible to cohere with the new requirements and precepts of the Counter-Reformation. In the process, the Catholic harmonisers, as Nicholas Watson puts it, 'necessarily disrupted the continuities and narrowed the range of the theologies on which they built ... transforming what had been a diverse series of arts of contemplation into a single, conceptually powerful science'.[28] It is unfortunately undeniable that many of those who have striven, over the centuries, to preserve ecclesiastical orthodoxy have felt more comfortable, when exerting their claims over the faithful, in travelling the reassuring and well-lit A-roads of certainty than the dark and threatening bridleways of ambiguity. Ironically, even a sanitised and authorised version of medieval mysticism, shorn of much of its long-haired, Carnaby Street radicalism, was too much for some. Watson continues: 'The place of mystical theology even within Catholic theology was always controversial. England's most prominent seventeenth-century mystic, Augustine Baker, for example, was read with suspicion after his death because of supposed echoes in his writing of Quietism, the condemned view that *unio mystica* (mystical union) involves a renunciation so complete that even the desire for God must be surrendered in order to attain him'.[29] A further example of suppression, or at least of well-intentioned censorship, can be found in the later writings of the revered Carmelite nun Thérèse of Lisieux (1873–97), whose biographical manuscripts published as *Story of a Soul* were deliberately tinkered with and sterilised by her prioress (and own sister) Mother Agnes so as to conform to conventional and idealised notions of nineteenth-century piety. Thérèse's agonies of loss, doubt and hope reveal a much more interesting, multi-layered and thoroughly ambivalent figure than the 'traditional simple nun'[30] known to Catholics as the 'Little Flower'. For Thérèse, the darkness is visible and it is all but absolute: 'When I sing of the happiness of heaven and of the eternal possession of God, I feel no joy in this, for I sing simply what I WANT TO BELIEVE. It is true that at times a very small ray of the sun comes to illumine my darkness, and then the trial ceases for *an instant*, but afterward the memory of this ray, instead of causing me joy, makes my darkness ever more dense'.[31] There can be few more poignant or powerful expressions than this of the mystic's deeply ambiguous and often frustrated path in establishing a relationship with divinity and experiencing lack of love or meaning.

The attractive but often troubling idea of the hiddenness of God has been addressed by a number of contemporary as well as medieval thinkers. For example, the late Ronald Thiemann, a former Bussey Professor of Historical Theology at Harvard University, quite recently developed a very subtle and intriguing idea, hinging on a notion of sacred immanence, of what he calls 'the humble sublime': of holiness present in the hidden. Locating continuity between theological and a number of diverse, nominally 'secular', writers, Thiemann suggests that God may be found not just where he might be expected to be, but also in his opposite. Discussing in turn Martin Luther, Dietrich Bonhoeffer, Albert Camus, George Orwell, Russian poet Anna Akhmatova and African-American poet Langston Hughes, Thiemann argues in favour – even in a thoroughly secularised and sceptical modern context, and contrary to the recent work of philosophers like Charles Taylor – of the idea of sacred worth and meaning as still having a vital part to play in the modern sense of the self. Thiemann writes as follows: 'Just as our salvation has been earned by the execution of a political prisoner in first-century Palestine, so also God's presence in our own times might be found where we are least likely to expect it, in those realms we too easily dismiss as the secular, mundane and unbelieving'.[32] By this reckoning, the everyday and the ordinary are redolent with mysterious depths: they contain a concealed spirituality, where for example heroic acts of courage, faith and resistance (such as resistance to political tyranny) are most perfectly realised in the mundane actions of 'ordinary' and 'humble' people. Though these ideas are far from being identical to the so-called 'anonymous Christianity' of the Roman Catholic theologian Karl Rahner – Thiemann himself was a Lutheran – they do appear to have some connectedness to, or at least bear interesting parallel with, what Rahner referred to in his Jesuitical systematic theology as a grace 'which always surrounds man, even the sinner and the unbeliever, as the inescapable setting of his existence'.[33]

But perhaps it is W. H. Vanstone, an Anglican clergyman, who has produced the most interesting idea – expressed via his classic and famous notion of dignified *waiting* – of the human relationship with God arriving not so much directly as surreptitiously and through concealment. For Vanstone, 'Waiting can be the most intense and poignant of all human experiences – the experience which, above all others, strips us of affectation and self-deception and reveals to us the reality of our needs, our values and ourselves'.[34] The whole point of such waiting is that something, usually something or someone that we earnestly desire – whether a lover, a wife, a new job, a salary rise or a foreign holiday – won't be given to us straightaway: or even in fact at all. This means that that something is, even if only temporarily, concealed from us. We can't access it. We can't hold it. It is absent. We have to come to terms with that fact – that we can't always get, or have, what we want; moreover, in that very interim, liminal process of waiting we are revealed in our full tragic dignity as mature human beings. Vanstone's perspective is a Christian one, directly related to Christ's waiting in the Garden of Gethsemane prior to the Passion. But it is an idea taken up by others with different beliefs and perspectives; for instance by Ursula Le Guin, in her splendid novel *The Left Hand of Darkness,* when she writes: 'It is good to have an end to journey towards; but it is the journey that matters, in the end'.[35] The process of getting somewhere may thus be more significant than reaching a final destination, even if the eventual safety or satisfaction of entering harbour is to be postponed.

The Left Hand of Darkness is strongly influenced by a Taoist philosophy of opposites, and patterns from ancient Chinese thought, which directly parallel the apophaticism of much medieval mysticism.[36] For this reason alone it deserves discussion within the same chapter as the Christian mystics. Dualities of light and darkness, yin and yang, are in fact everywhere in the book – most obviously in the androgyny of the planet's inhabitants, who are mostly neuter but at times exhibit the sexual and psychological characteristics of both female and male.[37] These binaries echo wider, existential polarities of darkness and light and are also, as Barbara Bucknell says, 'the reconciliation of opposites, conforming to each other's outline in perfect harmony.'[38] Superficially a work of science fiction, the novel exemplifies at a deeper level the compassionate humanity which characterises all the great works of this writer. Located on a planet called Gethin, or – appropriately – Winter (since the planet in question is held in the grip of a permanent ice-age), its plot centres on the efforts of an envoy from Earth, Genly Ai, to persuade the androgynes of this frozen world to join an interstellar union called the Ekumen. The Terran envoy is assisted in his efforts by the Prime Minister of Karhide, one of the competing two great powers of Winter, who is named Estraven. However, Estraven is toppled from power and exiled to nearby Orgoreyn. Genly Ai, disillusioned after his rejection by Argaven, the King of Karhide, tries his luck in the neighbouring country instead, but is thrown into a labour camp after betrayal by the very Orgoreyn faction that had first supported him and his objectives. Estraven dramatically rescues Genly, and the two of them escape from his captors and betrayers across the brutal ice fields that link Karhide and Orgoryen at their narrowest, northern tips. Once they make landfall in Karhide, following a journey of extraordinary hardship, fellowship and intensity, the envoy contacts his orbiting ship and its crew make preparations to descend to Winter. As news breaks of their imminent arrival, the Karhide government is persuaded to join the Ekumen, but not before the proscribed Estraven is gunned down by border guards in a doomed attempt to cross back into Orgoreyn. The envoy, who since has developed much love and admiration for Estraven, is numbed by the loss of his friend, despite the final success of his mission.

Such a bald summary does less than justice to the remarkable philosophy at the centre of the book, which is fundamentally – even as it explores dichotomised questions of love and loss – a celebration of uncertainty. Tormented by doubts as to whether or not Gethin will ever join the inter-planetary alliance, the envoy at one point consults a cult of foretellers called the Handdarata, whose mystical, oracular and trance-like divination of the future is entered into only reluctantly and with serious qualifications.[39] Though he is able to reassure Genly that his mission will succeed, the chief diviner, Faxe, is very clear that the foretellers themselves avoid answers whenever they can, and retreat to their Fastness 'mostly to learn what questions not to ask'.[40] The reason for this, as Faxe explains, is that 'the unforetold, the unproven, that is what life is based on.'[41] He continues: 'Ignorance is the ground of thought. Unproof is the ground of action. If it were proven that there is no God there would be no religion ... There's really only one question that can be answered ... and we already know the answer ... The only thing that makes life possible is permanent, intolerable uncertainty: not knowing what comes next'.[42] In this novel, perhaps the most brilliant and artistically realised expression of her own Taoist philosophy, Le Guin expresses the important idea not only that the mysteries of the universe are best discussed in terms of opposites – light, darkness; female, male; fear, courage – but also that the richness of life, in all its possibility, is absolutely dependent not on certainty, but on doubt. It is our encounter with the unknown that shapes us into the people we are.

Before my marriage ruptured I thought my own journey was complete, at least in its fundamentals. My wife and I settled in Norfolk in order to remain there. There was no thought on my part of starting over. But when our relationship collapsed all sense of meaning and purpose for a while went with it. What I have come to realise, in the years that have passed since, is that my sea-crossing, my voyage to new shores, was only just beginning. God can seem utterly remote, when we are suddenly hit by affliction. The devastating departure of a spouse; the parent who is struck down by illness; the sense of being suffocated by a life that no longer seems your own, or over which you feel you have no control – these are things that many of us have experienced, or may well experience in the future. But the accompanying alienation from any sense of transcendent presence, the doubt that may flood all available horizons, is not necessarily the end. It is a fair walk from Holkham village, along Lady Anne's Drive, down to the shore. Sometimes the scudding waves seem so distant that they appear a mere sliver: flatline of flickering blue or grey on an ever-receding skyline. It is possible to wonder, then, given the quixotic nature of the sands, and the serpentine runnels of water as they cascade treacherously down to the beach, if it is possible to reach the sea at all. But it is there. You just have to walk towards it to find it. And then keep walking, because it is the journey – of doubt, of disappointment, of deep uncertainty of what is at the end of it – that matters, in the end.

Chapter Three

ENDURANCE

Look out, over there, to the place where the sea meets the sky. Where the horizon ripples and gleams and beckons. It seems impossibly far and elusive. Ten thousand years ago, at this highest point on the Norfolk coast, there would have been no water in sight. The coastline lay fifty miles distant, and East Anglia met the continent in a land bridge. Here at Roman Camp, this breezy escarpment perched three hundred and fifty feet above the shore, my feet rest one evening on the precarious edge of prehistory. This is Norfolk's Switzerland: an improbable North Face, a tiny Eiger deposited in a county famous for its flatness. But as darkness deepens, and I take in the view of tree and sea, my modest hillock assumes an epic profile. Outcrop of the Cromer Ridge, this diminutive concentration of sands and gravel – abandoned at last by a retreating glacier – is the remnant of an ice sheet a thousand metres high. Sinking at last, the sun sears the edges of careering clouds in a fading carnival of amber. I inhale the scented air of medieval upland that once was more ancient forest. Still further back, this gentle knoll was as wild as any place on earth: feral up-country stalked by bears and sabre-toothed *cats. It is a mound as old as memory. It is a place of loss. Beneath my eyrie, underneath the waves, lies the ruined town of Shipden, fatal victim to erosion and storm. Now there are no wild beasts; and perhaps only Black Shuck, or Shukr – mythic dog-companion to Thor and his Norsemen – continues to haunt this lonely hill; alongside my own demons of hurt and grief. I clench my fists against recollection. We came here together often, you and I. Yet for all the pain, it brings me comfort. I can hear nightjars among the birches; and a solitary nightingale is singing from a blackthorn. Though darkness is upon me, I am surrounded by a luminous sea of heather: wave upon wave of purple in the swiftly gathering dusk. Away from tump and heathland, primeval trackways dive through gorse and bracken to secret, secluded places: perhaps to Bronze Age barrows where people buried their dead.*

Where are the dodging and laughing children, careering helter-skelter through the town? Where the cart-borne traffic, the shriek of pigs slaughtered in the yard, the braying of protesting donkeys who resist their masters' onerous baggage, or the putridity of effluent running in the lane? Where the crackle of fire and angry hiss of steam issuing from the forge, or the rhythmic slap, slap of hands and fingers easing and massaging tough hide into shape in the mephitic cockpit of the tannery? Between gates and woods, hills and lokes, were the people who make each single place unique. Black Friars and Grey Friars travelled alike to Shipden: cassocked and competing rivals in the marketplace, preaching the way to salvation on the great feast-days of Michaelmas and Corpus Christi. Bantering fisherwomen returned at evening through the Seagate laden with rattling bags of cockles for their stews, prized sea-borne booty; while all around – an inescapable miasma – lay the rank, heavy-laden stink of herring and cod. The silenced hubbub of these gabled, half-timbered streets rises out of the rock-pools of the past like so many wriggling krill; and like a fish hooked on a line I am ensnared and caught fast. Their medieval voices come back to me now: the cries of those trapped in the deeps.

From out of the grey waves, drawn to Shipden for trade or commerce, came travellers and mariners; in transit perhaps to the Baltic, possibly to the land of ice, or bound even for the Holy Land and the spice-laden Middle Sea. A dozen languages echoed through its streets and taverns: the robust northern German of traders in honey and fur from Danzig and Lübeck; guttural Flemish spoken by weavers from Bruges and Ghent, disembarked at Shipden to appraise the latest woolpacks from Lavenham; the melodic Gallo-Italic dialect of cloth-traders from Genoa; and a Norse tongue, sparse as an alpine spruce, uttered by dour fishermen hailing from Denmark and the untamed North Way. Here and there, on the slick surface of Shipden's quay, lie discarded fish-heads and the scattered detritus of maritime exchange: grey-green bottles, the latest Gascon vintage, glinting in piles in the sunlight; sacks of prized and pricy Cotswold wool, renowned for its quality and warmth, piled high beside the doors of a string of warehouses and wharves; and unkempt stacks of timber from some distant, mist-laden Prussian forest. As seagulls scream and dive into the wind, salt mingles with the pungent whiff of caulk and tar. Beneath heavy mooring rings, parading up and down the brick-and-flint jetty like so many attentive eyes, are assembled English cogs, Genoese galleys and Hansard barques: a tapestry of bobbing barrels, ready to be rolled away to destinations of terror and risk.

The sea, the sea: I can hear it sigh as it washes against the portals of my mind, as if in lament for a life short-lived. What stories does it bring, the surf that lashes the vanished shore of Shipden? As a northeasterly whips around the curving Blakeney headland, and tidal waves tower above the broken cliffs, spattering the tumbled bricks of ruined inns and abbeys with frenzied spume, I fancy I can hear the voices of the drowned, those souls long-lost and captured by the waves, their lives and dreams pummelled into as many splinters as the planks and timbers of their far-sighted brigs. Forever hungry, the sea has taken them. No longer shall the mariners of memory jest by the quay as they boast to their girls of voyages to some distant gulf. No more do the ships' masters set their compasses against the stars, as Capella, Sirius and Rigel chart their own mysterious courses across the speckled heavens. While constellations shed starlight upon the lid of a settling ocean, far below, in the winter deeps, I catch distant murmurings. Once it was said here that mermaids laugh merrily and toss their hair as one by one they count on their webbed fingers the graves of dead men.

Into my heart an air that kills
   From yon far country blows:

What are those blue remembered hills,
   What spires, what farms are those?

That is the land of lost content,
   I see it shining plain,

The happy highways where I went
   And cannot come again.

A. E. Housman, *A Shropshire Lad*

If all our lives are journeys – fragmentary, frequently unmapped and often conducted with compass broken – there is one part of it that for me stands out in memory. There is a particular path that curves around the foot of Incleborough Hill, between the north Norfolk villages of East and West Runton, where quite suddenly field and hedgerow give way to untrammelled sea views. A sudden smudge of blue becomes a much larger theatre of azure in a yet wider setting of beet, barley and wheat. Living nearby, I was able to enjoy this panorama on an almost weekly basis. It was not exactly dramatic in its impact, being too serene for epic landscape. (Incleborough is no Helvellyn.) But in its tranquil and ordered aggregation of proper Norfolk hedgerow, yellow gorse and festival of wild-flowers – milk-parsley, wood-sedge, sand-sedge, Breckland thyme, malted sea-lavender and the prized umbel-like clusters of an occasional Star of Bethlehem, that delicate white perennial of the dry East Anglia grassland – it somehow was quintessentially and pleasingly English. I came to associate my walks here with a kind of uncomplicated happiness. It made me realise in an intensely felt and deeply personal way how much a cherished topography like this can help you start to feel part of something greater than yourself. It was perhaps a similar sense of transcendent connectedness to landscape, and a comparable glimpse of another distant patch of blue, which prompted that master of Arcadian landscape-writing, John Cowper Powys, to reflect in one of his novels, and in markedly elegiac terms, of an 'entrance to some great highway of the ether, whose air-spun pavement was not the colour of dust, but the colour of turquoise'.[1] For Powys' character Wolf, a character into which the novelist has poured so much of his own idiosyncratic pantheism, that 'incredible patch of blue seemed something into which he could plunge his hands and draw them forth again, filled like overflowing cups with the very ichor of happiness'.[2] This brings with it keen philosophical insight, a sort of pastoral eureka moment: 'Ah! That was the word. It was *pure happiness*, that blue patch!'[3] It is of its nature that uncomplicated happiness rarely if ever lasts, and that is precisely why, when we do experience it, it has the joyous impact of something revelatory.

But even a place as placid and uplifting as this can be temperamental. Quite suddenly a squall blows in off the North Sea, and the mood and atmosphere of this halcyon setting shift direction in a manner as swift as it is complete. The sky darkens, as if focusing and accumulating all of its elemental and antagonistic power; and the sea, previously so bright and inviting, seethes with concentrated rage as its breakers unleash themselves in an assault of furious white spindrift against the strandline. It is then that the east wind blows at its most malign, and with it comes the sense that this coast has always struggled against the risk of loss. It can be beautiful, yes. But its natural beauty has always been conjoined with danger. Attractiveness and ferocity form the inseparable bipolarity of a shore that likes nothing better than to smash those who venture into its protean waters. Its longsuffering people have always had to practise endurance. Those whose descendants now inhabit the settlements once called Wiventona, Claia, Esnuterle, Salhus and Guella[4] felt far from sentimental about villages that came to be known, thanks to the later writings of Clement Scott, as Poppyland. This was a coast that consumed whole families, which devastated communities. The spectral and impenetrable smoke of its drifting sea-frets seemed the sinister harbinger of far-off maritime disaster. Sailors sometimes never returned from the icy Baltic sea-roads. The storms that erased the wayfarers of the seas also ate up entire towns. Cosmopolitan and powerful Dunwich, once 'the sixth greatest town of England',[5] is the best known but by no means the only example of a settlement or port whose haunting remnants tell of a medieval society literally blown away by wave and storm. And it's then that happiness gives way to a sense of loss and ruin – for with an appreciation of the charms of the landscape between the Runtons, clustered around an Incleborough Hill liberally swathed in vibrant moss and heather, comes realisation that just a mile out to sea lies the submerged town of Shipden-juxta-Mare. Local folklore had it that only a fool would take to the waters if the bells of Shipden Church could be heard from beneath the waves, for it was then a thing as certain as sunrise that a storm was on the way.

In the fourteenth century Shipden was a thriving town with a busy harbour and several manors, among them one owned by the Paston family (of eponymous letters fame) and another in the possession of the crown. However, we know that by 1337 the sea had done very considerable damage to the doomed port.[6] Shipden's church, dedicated to St Peter, was abandoned by the early 1340s, while its deracinated population was forced to migrate inland to the satellite settlement of Crowsmere. In his fascinating account of the vanished communities of the Norfolk coast, published in 2006, Neil Storey claims that all the fishermen of the area remain aware of the lost village, which stood on the seaward side of the town that we know today as Cromer. Indeed, Church Rock, just beyond the famous pier, remains a hazard to shipping. Storey writes: 'On 9 August 1888 the pleasure steamer *Victoria* had set out on an unwise course from the pier when her hull scraped over Church Rock and was holed on her port side. Fortunately, she did not sink and all passengers were ferried off and sent home by train. Surely this is the only instance of a ship being stranded on top of a church tower!'[7] He cites in support the *Norfolk Directory* written by William White in 1890: 'At very low tides there are still to be seen, nearly half a mile from the cliffs, large masses of wall, composed of square flints, which sailors call church rock'.[8]

There is much to be gained, I feel, from reflecting on the resilience and courage of these coastal communities whose streets and houses – whose inns, trades and church towers – were over time pounded into fragments by the encroaching waves. These were individuals for whom perseverance and sufferance were their daily bread. In the end the places they were born, the lanes they had played and lived in, were taken from them as surely and inevitably as their own short and difficult lives were subject to termination. The Norfolk coast is now rightly popular with holidaymakers, but few visitors, thankfully, will know the terror of sailors and fishermen who had to steer their craft away from the menacing Haisbro' Sands, known to generations of mariners as the Devil's Throat, near Happisburgh; or fully appreciate the hardship of fishing communities who tried to eke a living from crab, lobster, whiting, cod and salt herring. This was a faithful community, for which Christianity and the hope of resurrection served as guiding lights in the storm. But it was also an anxious and sometimes fearful one. Furthermore, for all the courage of heroic life-boatmen like the later – and rightly celebrated – Henry Blogg (1876–1954),[9] it was not always generous. The medieval men of Wells, or Guella, had a reputation for plunder and wreck and earned the sobriquet 'bitefingers' for their unsavoury method of removing rings from the digits of drowned sailors. If you look carefully today at the interior walls of Wiveton and Salthouse churches you can see etched there, into the medieval stonework, the graffiti of miniature boats carved by mariners. Perhaps this was done in the earnest hope that they and their ships would be protected by the magical efficacy of ancient prayer and liturgy. There was no guarantee of safety from either storm or wreckers; but there was hope, even in the midst of grave uncertainty about long-term survival in the tempest, and of whatever dangers lay ahead during the voyage.

Julia Blackburn, who shows a deep understanding of the connection between seashore and magic, between mystery and ambiguity, evokes the continuing dangers of this coast in her book about the Sheringham fisherman turned invalid embroiderer, John Craske. Blackburn attempts to get to the bottom of the life and times of the elusive Craske, who fell seriously ill – probably from untreated diabetes – in 1917, aged thirty-six, and then in 1923 began to produce a series of remarkable and richly detailed embroideries of the sea (culminating in his masterpiece *The Evacuation of Dunkirk*, completed after the improbable rescue of the British Expeditionary Force from the beaches of Normandy). The author's investigation of an individual segues into a searching meditation on the very nature of change and incertitude. It is also a moving testament to a fragile faith in the future. In examining a number of Craske's embroideries at Snape Maltings, in nearby Suffolk, Blackburn sees in them something revelatory, as well as profoundly true: 'I cannot begin to explain how much the pictures impressed me', she writes. 'They were images of the sea and boats on the sea and the coast seen from a boat, but they were also images of life itself and its precariousness and how we struggle to keep afloat and to stay alive in the face of fear and uncertainty. All these fragile vessels: tossed by waves and sometimes almost engulfed by them, out there in the vastness of the ocean. Some were pinpointed by the angled glare of a lighthouse like the eye of God staring straight at them, others had smoke billowing from their funnels as they tried to plough their way through a storm. I had the sense at once that it was all true: the tilt of a boat in relation to the swell of the waves and the strength of the wind: the rigging, the billowing of the sails.'[10] Craske's work then becomes a metaphor, as the book continues, for the changes about to break, like a dark and stormy wave, over the life of the author herself. Indeed, this affecting and poignant book, which – echoing its own subject – is constructed as a kind of tapestry of inter-stitched meditations and reflections, ends with the unexpected death in their Suffolk garden of Blackburn's eighty-year-old partner, Herman. In reaching the end of both book and era ('the nature of the world I inhabited had changed irrevocably'[11]), the author admits that she didn't know when she started her project, or even at the moment of completion, if her subject, John Craske, was a significant artist or not. But it doesn't, she feels, matter either way: 'his work made his life meaningful for him and he went on doing it, almost to the moment of his death.'[12] This realisation pulls the author towards the final words of her book, where full acknowledgement is made of 'life and death and love and loss'.[13] In deciding to pursue and persevere with her subject, despite ambivalence about the value of Craske's legacy, and in the face of her own acute and recent bereavement, these are words that, as she says, 'keep me moving forward step by step into the future.'[14] Doubt is thus for Julia Blackburn not a brake on what is to follow. It results in a tentatively hopeful capacity to face what life, in all its cruel uncertainty, yet may bring the author's way.

Doubt and faith go hand in hand on the Norfolk coast. The malign east wind, that sweeps unimpeded across the North Sea, sometimes from as far away as the Ural Mountains, is forever gusting; but its maleficent effects are offset by those warmer, gentler winds that blow from inland, across the Brecks and beyond. With characteristic lyricism, but climatic and meteorological accuracy, John Cowper Powys writes as follows:[15] 'In a country like East Anglia so peculiarly at the mercy of the elements, every one of the winds has its own peculiar burden and brings with it something healing and restorative or baleful and malefic. The east wind here is, in a paramount sense, the evil wind, the accomplice and confederate of the salt deep, the blighter of hopes, the herald of disaster. The north-west wind, on the contrary, is the wind that brings the sense of inland spaces, the smell of warm, wet earth and the fragrance of leaf-mould in sweet breathing woods. It is the wind that fills the rivers and the wells and brings the fresh purifying rain. It is a wind full of memories and its heart is strong with the power of ancient love, revived even out of graves and sepulchres'.[16] For Powys 'earth, not sea is man's proper habitation',[17] while justifiable horror of the ocean is countered by the calming recollection of beautiful East Anglian gardens. As one commentator has remarked, the prevailing quality of this Norfolk novel is dramatic throughout – more so perhaps than the later Wessex books. The sea is sinister and its tides godless. Moreover, 'the desolate fens strike terror. Nature's malignancy expresses itself in dark clouds, pitiless winds and a weird storm.'[18] Yet the scent of fragrant earth is able to drive away the lingering evil of the deeps. Powys well understands the topography of the eastern counties, where storm and rain, lightning and sunshine, thunder and fog can all manifest within moments; many is the time I have been drenched on a sunlit beach at Holkham by some sudden and ferocious scud. He knows too that both types of wind – east and north-western – are integral to the essential character of the place. Just so faith and uncertainty.

The huge popularity in East Anglia of the Book of Hours, a Latin prayer-book used for private devotion[19] (often by women) during the Middle Ages, at first suggests that the spiritual seedbed of the region was that of fairly a conventional pious religiosity. Drawing their material overwhelming from the Psalter, these medieval scriptural manuals (which include The Marston Hours, produced in East Anglia around 1250, and the Fenlands De Veres Hours illuminated some sixty years later) chiefly contained biblical texts with illustrations reflecting on scenes from the infancy and Passion of Christ. However, they were also crammed full of extra-biblical material – as Eamon Duffy puts it 'suffrages to and images of the saints, litanies, indulgenced prayers to the wounds of Jesus, to the Blessed Sacrament, to the Virgin Mary'.[20] It is no great surprise that these medieval manuals later became one of the bitter battlegrounds of the Reformation, since the women and men who copied supplications and commentary into their prayer-books were concerned with suspicious matters that were anathema to the new Protestantism: for example, with 'prayers which carried indulgences, or legends guaranteeing spiritual or material benefits, especially protection against life's troubles and the terrors of death'.[21] It is perhaps no huge exaggeration to say that, until Cranmer's reforms took hold, people in the Middle Ages employed prayer books much as people today use smartphones: to gain access to information that would be of use to them in guiding their way through the pitfalls and pressures of life. They wanted practical results, though of course as much with a view to the life to come as with their preoccupations and interests in the present. As Duffy says, 'Late medieval people collected prayers as we collect recipes, and for rather similar reasons'.[22]

A further core component of the Book of Hours was the Office of the Dead,[23] and it is here that we see a much less confident and upbeat spirituality. Duffy detects here 'deeper and more sombre notes' with the Office's Psalms 'adding the themes of desolation and supplication to those of hope and confidence so dominant in the Hours of the Virgin'.[24] He continues: 'Alongside "The Lord is my shepherd", and "I love the Lord, for he has heard the cry of my appeal", the Office of the Dead was also an urgent supplication: "Out of the depths I have cried to thee O Lord". The magnificent readings from the Book of Job which formed the heart of Matins for the Dead probed even deeper, filled as they are with reproach and appeal to God, rooted in the sense of human fragility and suffering, the brevity of life and the bitterness of death – "Man that is born of woman hath but a short time to live, and is full of troubles", "Have mercy on me O God, for my days are nothing"'.[25] It is clear from these prayer-books that medieval belief was never a matter to be taken for granted. It involved a difficult, challenging and testing relationship with the divine which took the believer into places where a sense of the transcendent was often hard to find. Finitude, the bitter taste of mortality, hardship and loss were ever-present companions on life's journey. This resulted in a rich and resonant spirituality that was far from simplistic or resistant to subtle interrogation of what human beings were here for.

As Graeme Smith has remarked, the Middle Ages are often seen as golden age for Christianity: a pious era of untroubled belief and universal worship. The usual picture is that the Enlightenment changed all that; and it was after the *Aufklärung* that atheism and anti-clericalism emerged as really significant intellectual and cultural forces. By this reckoning, it was the Age of Reason that pushed religion out of public life and into the realm of public opinion. However, Smith thinks contrarily that 'The religious activity of the Middle Ages was highly complex, by no means universally Christian and devout in any sense we would recognise today'.[26] While for Eamon Duffy religion was alive and meaningful in every segment of society, for Smith 'Medieval religious behaviour is in fact very similar to that in the contemporary West. What we have today is minority religious activism, the 15 per cent or so who attend church, alongside majority passive Christian support, the 70 per cent and more who claim some sort of Christian identity and express a vague desire for the idea of a God. Medieval Christianity was the same. A minority were very serious about their Christianity, whilst a majority were supportive but from a distance. They did not want to make Christianity the centre of their lives, but nor did they want to challenge or abandon it'.[27] I suspect that, as is often the way, the truth lies somewhere in the middle. The majority were in fact devout, and happy to go to church; they did not have a worldview which presented any coherent alternative. But belief did not prevent them from asking extremely pointed questions of a God whom they felt had treated them badly, left them behind or who vacated himself from their prayers.

After my marriage broke up it became clear over time that I would not be able to remain in the home my absent wife and I had shared. But our Norfolk house was distinctive and unconventional and, at the beginning of a localised housing slump, not easy to sell. In the midst of all the grief, disappointment and disconnection that so often accompany the end of a longish and familiar partnership there was nevertheless the miserable business to negotiate of attempting to arrange a sale – as well as deal with all the other practicalities of marital disengagement. While autumn gales gave way to winter storms, and rain battered at the windows of my empty and echoing home, I tried to take some comfort in reflecting on the travails of all the afflicted people who had lived before me on the coast, and who in their own ways had endured hurt and loss. Though it is often said that every breakup feels different, and perhaps that is true, finding myself precipitately alone was not of course a unique experience. It is absolutely part of being human to have to face up to the end of things, usually in ways we cannot predict or anticipate or control. Death – whether an actual death, or the agonising demise of that which we loved and trusted and depended on – may come quickly or slowly, but it is still only a raised latch away in the adjoining room. My own world seemed to have splintered apart at the roots, yet any metaphorical talk of things crumbling to dust or ashes hardly reflected the realities of depredated communities, such as the one at Shipden, which had had in the past to confront the loss of hearth, home and even life. To distract myself from the pain I threw myself into work; but time spent at home still dragged like the useless arm of a shell-shocked man who shuffles around while nursing a mortal wound – which I felt truly to be the case. I made friends with my neighbour Joe, recently widowed, whose wife Judith had died shockingly in his arms just minutes before the ambulance had been able to reach her. Together we sat up late, drank wine and whisky and talked of the spouses we had known and loved. During this period, for all my friend's humanity and sensitive interest, without which I might not have come to shore, I had considerable doubt that I would again recover my equilibrium. Depression was hard to keep at bay. I felt lost on an uncharted ocean of darkness. I had no map, no plan, no safe haven and no way of reaching harbour. The idea of God seemed almost impossibly far away. There was perhaps after all no high benignity in the universe, at least the one I now inhabited. The only true eternity lay in the deeps, the chasm into which I had fallen. For the first time I felt that I knew, not just in my head but in my heart, the devastation so trenchantly articulated, across the gulfs of time, by the writer of Psalm 13:

> *'How long will this pain go on, Lord,*
> *   this grief I can hardly bear?*
>
> *How long will anguish grip me*
> *   and agony wring my mind?*
>
> *Light up my eyes with your presence;*
> *   let me feel your love in my bones.*
>
> *Keep me from losing myself*
> *   in ignorance and despair.*
>
> *Teach me to be patient, Lord;*
> *   teach me to be endlessly patient.*
>
> *Let me trust that your love enfolds me*
> *   when my heart feels desolate and dry.*
>
> *I will sing to the Lord at all times,*
> *   even from the depths of pain.'*[28]

Singing seemed a very unlikely eventuality, though certainly there was to be pain a-plenty. But as dry days turned into parched weeks and then those endless weeks somehow connected up into whole months, despair gave way slowly to a determination to make it through. I had loved; I had lost; but I was not finished. I began to see friends again. I was able to contemplate a future. The very fact of enduring the pain seemed somehow to have robbed it of its capacity to take me down. I began to think more deeply about what starting again might mean – not just in practical terms, though certainly that too, but also existentially. It was clear that a new beginning was going to involve at least some measure of absence from the region I loved. A complete break from the places she and I had gone together, and lived in together, seemed imperative. I began to read the psalms again, just as those who possessed a Book of Hours might have done, and concentrated especially on those passages about the yearning of the departed for a relinquished but deeply cherished land. In 597 BCE the Jerusalem of rebellious vassal King Jehoiachim fell to the Neo-Babylonian armies of Nebuchadnezzar II, and the Temple of Yahweh was sacked. Ten years later the holy city was attacked and razed by the same armies, and up to a quarter of the city's populace deported to Babylon, by then again the dominant power in the Ancient Near East. Psalm 13, quoted above, and the similarly anguished Psalm 102, may well date from the period of the Babylonian Exile, when the children of Israel were forcibly uprooted and the trauma of displacement began truly to bite. The most famous of all the psalms of exile is 137:

> '*By the waters of Babylon,*
> *there we sat down and wept,*
> *when we remembered Zion.*

> *On the willows there*
> *we hung our lyres.*

> *For there our captors*
> *required of us songs,*
> *and our tormenters, mirth, saying,*

> *"Sing us one of the songs of Zion!"*

> *How shall we sing the Lord's song*
> *in a foreign land?*

> *If I forget you, O Jerusalem,*

> *let my right hand wither!*'[29]

The psalmists knew in an immediate and personal way, in their own direct and seismic exposure to loss and longing, what it is like to have to give up that which you love beyond measure; and what it is like to yearn for that to which you can no longer have access or touch or physically experience. They speak of pain; and of a sorrow they think will never be extinguished. Many of the most memorable psalms are joyful hymns of praise, and these can be immensely beautiful: full of life, vitality and vividly drawn colour. But the verses which resonate best with me are those which speak of the agonies of separation; of shame or humiliation; of final divorce from an adored land that can never again be reclaimed. Any prolonged engagement with the biblical psalms makes you realise that there are no easy answers here; and nor do the psalmists think that there should be. These are texts filled to the brim with despair and doubt about what the future may hold. They are very often angry with God. And they are all the more powerful and authentic – and above all human – in consequence. Their voices carry the same cadences as that of J. L. Carr, who puts it so well in another context: 'We can ask and ask, but we can't have again what once seemed ours for ever – the way things looked, that church alone in the fields, a bed on a belfry floor, a remembered voice, the touch of a hand, a loved face. They've gone and you can only wait for the pain to pass'.[30] Yet for all that pain accompanies our lives, we so often take life itself for granted; and while we hold on to life, swept up in the moment of living, it seems somehow inexhaustible. But that which seeps unstoppably away from us – the spilt and passing moments described so well by Carr – is the very stuff of mortality: evaporating seconds both sweet and bitter. Bittersweet is the sight of an approaching raincloud on Gun Hill above the sands at Holkham; bittersweet the remembered touch of a lover long departed. There will be no cloud exactly like that again; no new kiss like that last one; and every blade of grass at our feet is singular. The precious nanoseconds we hold are the eternities we instantly lose. That simultaneity is the poignant paradox of who we are: our glory is our holding and our not holding, our gaining and our relinquishing. Propelled by the mysterious and implacable imperative of existence,[31] we are born and we die from instant to instant. It is the very uncertainty of whether the ground will hold firm beneath us that in the end pushes us forwards to test the weight of our boots on the dune.

In the knowledge that my time on the coast, at least as a Norfolk resident, was drawing to an end, I began to revisit some of the land and seascapes that had meant so much to me in years past. The awareness of approaching separation seemed to provide me with some armour against memories bound up with those places that I might previously have found to be unendurable. I walked again up Roman Camp, and looked over a seafront that at one time had not been there at all. I strode out on the sea wall at Burnham Overy Staithe and considered the dangerously alluring island of Scolt Head (or just 'the Island'), separated from the mainland by a mere seventy feet of placid seeming water: but in reality as perilous and Janus-faced as any stretch of shore in Norfolk. I set off up Gramborough Hill, site of a third-century Romano-British settlement which rises above Salthouse Heath, and thought of a salt tang on the wind, of flint eroded from upper chalk, of sea-campion and sea-bindweed, of hidden underworlds of cockle and mussel beds and of spring tides as they lapped over threatened and submerging reed beds. I sat for an hour in the cool and silent space of the priory at lonely Binham,[32] contemplating the bare walls of a church whose once brightly decorated murals were covered with lime-washed plaster. I examined there the remains of Binham's rood screen, torn down at the Reformation and encased now for posterity in glass, which depicted Christ as the Man of Sorrows.[33] Affecting and moving in its simple, unadorned humanity, it had been crudely overpainted with a Gothic script reproduced from Cranmer's prayer book of 1539. But for all their iconoclastic zeal, the Reformers – at least here at Binham – had signally failed in their goal: like unbidden yet solemn and determined ghosts, the unmistakeable forms of the original patristic saints were materialising spectrally through the later flaking paintwork. Even as I sat in misery, filled with a sense of deprivation – of the forfeiture of wife, home and profoundly loved landscape – it was again brought home to me that the transcendent may be present as much in the hidden as the revealed. Perhaps God did not want me to find him in the immediate or the facile or the obvious. There is truth and beauty to be found on the byways as much as on the highways of belief. Here, made manifest after centuries of concealment, were remarkable images of medieval piety that no Reformer could bear to see. Pictorial illustration had in the sixteenth century been supplanted by the Word of God. Yet the saints, despite all hostile efforts to erase them, had returned. I took this as an encouraging sign: that perhaps, for all that things had not gone my way, I too had the capacity to stage a comeback. In the meantime all I had to do was acknowledge the loss, just as the psalmists had, of the life and love that I had wrongly thought were mine. Though it was right to doubt that things might always fall out well, it was also right and proper to hold out hope for redemption. The author of Psalm 102, for all the agony of loss, had looked also to the future:

> 'You rebuild the desolate city;
>   you bring the exiles back home.
>
> You grant the poor your abundance;
>   you guide the nations toward peace.
>
> You hear the cry of the destitute
>   and the sobbing of the oppressed.
>
> You soothe the pain of the captive;
>   you set the prisoner free.'[34]

The wilderness of coastal north Norfolk possesses a solitariness and a melancholy beauty all of its own that cannot I think be replicated. It is not a spectacular landscape, even if it is a primal, reticent and fascinating one. But in preparing to leave it, I was brought to mind of the French travel writer Sylvain Tesson, who for six months in 2010 – the year my wife and I bought our coastal home – lived in a rudimentary hut, altogether alone, in the icy wastes of Siberia alongside the looming depths of prehistoric and dramatic Lake Baikal. Six months into his monastic and Thoreau-like vigil, with only bears, birds and occasional foresters and trappers for company, Sylvain received a five-line text message via his emergency satellite phone that his girlfriend had determined to leave him. Later on that evening, overcome by grief and exhausted by weeping, he records in his journal that a seal broke through the ice, in front of the beach adjacent to his lonely shack. The sight of it prompts the distraught writer to wonder, half-seriously, if the animal is in fact the woman he loved, 'come to smile at me ... I must manage to speak to her one last time'.[35] As Tesson suggests, the opportunity for appropriate or final words doesn't always present itself, when relationships go irrevocably awry. ('Time doesn't hand out second chances.'[36]) The freedom to love is always counterpointed by the freedom to leave, while love itself constitutes the ultimate voyage of doubt. However well that you think that you know someone, however much you think they are uniquely recognisable, no close companion is ever understood in their entirety. That is because human beings are not problems to be solved but mysteries to be cherished and appreciated – even at great personal cost and risk. Like Baikal, we all have hidden depths which can never be clearly seen. Perhaps those depths are blurry and indistinct, even to ourselves. We don't know exactly when or where our feet will touch bottom. Most icebergs show us only their tips, not the massive stumps that extend hundreds or even thousands of feet into the water and which will never break its numbing and glacial surface. What's swimming down there in the abyss may not be what we want to find. For the abandoned Tesson, the silence of his isolation has in previous days led to a kind of personal epiphany, where even mundane, everyday things become holy and sanctified: 'Light ennobles all it touches even glancingly: wood, the row of books, the knife handles, the curve of a face and of time going by, even the dust motes in the air'. This leads him to reflect that 'that's not nothing, to be specks of dust in this world'.[37] Such revelations do not however lead to belief, and the writer is quick to reject any notion of a personal faith: 'Strange, this need for transcendence. Why believe in a God outside His own creation? The crackling of the ice, the gentleness of the titmice, and the puissance of the mountains stir me more than any idea of the master of these ceremonies. They are enough for me. If I were God, I would atomise myself into millions of facets so I could dwell in ice crystals, cedar needles, the sweat of women, the scales of potted char, and the eyes of the lynx. More exhilarating than floating about in infinite space, watching from afar as the blue planet self-destructs'.[38] Such joyous celebration of immanence is a salutary reminder that the experience of landscape and loss is invariably ambiguous. It is always individual and it is forever distinct. We might take comfort in the natural world, when confronted with sudden absence – even a world so badly threatened by pollution and precipitate warming. We might find solace for our loneliness in the snow that covers the conifers on the mountains, or the first flowers of spring or the inquisitive seal that reminds us of the attentions of departed lover or friend. But not all pathways lead to divinity. For some, there is only an absence in the heart that can never be filled, or a hut in the woods beside a spring that is always brackish. Such experiences are as compellingly authentic and valid as their contrary faith-based counterparts.

Ursula Le Guin, most humane and wise of authors, writes in one of her novels that 'Freedom is a great and strange burden for the spirit to undertake. It is not easy. It is not a gift given, but a choice made, and the choice may be a hard one. The road goes upward towards the light; but the laden traveller may never reach the end of it'.[39] In choosing the freedom to hope we are also embracing the freedom to doubt that there is any real certainty or positivity ahead for us. There are no sureties on the long roads to fulfilment. Yet that does not mean there are not also destinations worth getting to. Faith in the future, in some outcome as yet unseen, but nevertheless ardently to be hoped for, may involve creative agnosticism, and considerable incertitude. It may involve moments of abjectness. It may at times mean cursing God. It may even mean denying God. Many people of faith have experienced moments of abandonment, even in the end of negation. The flight of Peter from Gethsemane is not sui generis. But to give oneself permission to doubt, to raise fundamental and difficult questions about religious ultimacy, does not mean embracing the absence of all transcendent meaning in the universe – or asserting that, despite the setbacks we suffer, and the many awful things that we have to endure, that wider things have no spiritual pregnancy at all.

The point about doubt is that if you care enough about a relationship with divinity, whatever that may involve, and then question the legitimacy and veracity of these relations without opting for a permanent or wholesale rejection – which already suggests a measure of open-mindedness to an opposing outcome – then things must to some degree *matter*. They must be worth having some hesitancy or uncertainty *about*. Jesus thought himself finally abandoned by God in the doubt and dark dereliction of a humiliating death intended for a criminal. This was perhaps, as he conceived it, the ultimate betrayal and desertion. But the Christian story, or at least the ongoing story of the founder's religion, did not end there – or with his cry 'Eloi, Eloi, lama sabachthani'. In the rich and painful hinterlands of religious ambiguity, there is, as we have seen, more than one road to the sea.

Chapter Four

REVIVAL

'Every real creation of art is independent, more powerful
than the artist himself, and returns to the divine through
its own manifestation. It is one with man only in this,
that it bears testimony to the mediation of the divine
within him.'

– Beethoven

*Padua, 1984: one of a visiting group of English art history
students, I gaze up at Giotto's empyrean. The murals of
the Scrovegni Chapel are as transporting as anything
I know that I have seen. The biblical stories brought to
life here extend far beyond themselves into an intense,
otherworldly dimension of light, feeling and contrast that
is impossible to name or to fathom. The painter's pigments
– vermilion, ultramarine, lazuline blue – glimmer and
glow in the intimate space of the capella like incandescent
jewels from the treasure of a doge. Mirabile: scenes that
catch at the heart, even as they seduce the eye, these images
will forever be burned into my memory. It comes to me
then that Italy may always mean this: the place where the
divine became possible; where God was made manifest in*

brushstrokes of gold leaf and tempera. On the train back to Venice, we are joined by local Italians. One of them, a girl of my own age, addresses me impulsively: What do you think of our Giotto? she asks. She seems to incarnate some essential kernel of being and vitality: perhaps it is the very quintessence of Italy. As our carriage hurtles through the villages of the Veneto, I know that I have had an epiphany: it is the beginning of a passion from which I wish never to be freed.

Padua, thirty years later: the day before my second marriage. I have returned to be transported by Giotto, to reflect on the mysterious workings of fate and the past. This will forever be my city now – città di Galileo Galilei. It is a town of clattering squares, of cafes and laughter, of churches and ciaos, of porticos and palazzi whose elegance, as you see embodied there the ideals and genius of its Renaissance creators, evokes unfailing wonder at its harmonies and symmetries. I sit often now, on that same train to Venice, with the woman who tomorrow is to become my wife. Graduate of Ca' Foscari, she has retained the Padovana's fierce pride: to her, the Venetians are foreigners. This is not the beginning of my journey, or even the end – rather the mid-point of a voyage that reconciles the past and the future: the dreams of a boy starting out with the aspirations of a middle-aged man. Giotto does not disappoint. In the man stirs the boy's rapture. He remains open to what is to come.

'I was utterly alone with the sun and earth. Lying down on the grass, I spoke in my soul to the earth, the sun, the air, and the distant sea far from sight. I thought of the earth's firmness – I felt it bear me up; through the grassy couch there came an influence as if I could feel the great earth speaking to me. I thought of the wandering air – its pureness, which is its beauty; the air touched me and gave me something of itself. I spoke to the sea: though so far, in my mind I saw it, green at the rim of the earth

*and blue in deeper ocean ... I turned to the blue heaven
over, gazing into its depth, inhaling its exquisite colour
and sweetness. The rich blue of the unattainable flower
of the sky drew my soul towards it, and there it rested,
for pure colour is rest of heart. By all these I prayed ...
Then, returning, I prayed by the sweet thyme, whose
little flowers I touched with my hand; by the slender
grass; by the crumble of dry chalky earth I took up and let
fall through my fingers. Touching the crumble of earth,
the blade of grass, the thyme flower, breathing the earth-
encircling air, thinking of the sea and the sky, holding out
my hand for the sunbeams to touch it, prone on the sward
in token of deep reverence, thus I prayed.'*

– Richard Jefferies (1848–87)

*'The worst of partialities is to withhold oneself, the worst
ignorance is not to act, the worst lie is to steal away.'*
– Charles Péguy

*'There is something mysterious in the universe which is
in complicity with those who love nothing but the good.'*
– Simone Weil

'How do you pick up the threads of an old life?' asks
Frodo rhetorically in Peter Jackson's film of J. R. R.
Tolkien's novel *The Return of the King*: 'how do you go on
when in your heart you begin to understand ... that there
is no going back?' Such questions seemed to me more
than usually pointed in the aftermath of divorce and
separation. Some close friendships in Norfolk remained
intact; but following the irrevocable loss of the wedding
ring, thrown into and unmade in the smoking caldera
of its own personalised Mount Doom, there seemed

little now to look forward to – or, for that matter, to hope for. The magic for me had gone out of the world. The conversations with friends that might once have stimulated and delighted now, without my wife to enjoy them with, seemed curiously flat and two-dimensional. The absence of our partnership had robbed them of some inner quality of life, joy and effervescence. Departure from the former marital home now became essential, and so I took a six-month lease on a basement flat in London to be closer to my work and distract myself from the things I had lost. As I surveyed this new and unforeseen cursed earth, the forty by forty square feet and the few possessions in it that had escaped storage and become my world, the devastation of losing my coastal home held me in a vice-like grip. This was perhaps the worst of times – one of confusions, of uncertainties around what I was doing and where my life was heading, and about where and how I wanted to live. As shock and grief gave way to leaden-hearted resignation, I started to know, not just emotionally and intellectually but in my innermost being, that life as I had imagined and understood it for the best part of a decade was now definitively, gut-rippingly, over. There was no marriage; there was no security; there were no parents-in-law, trips or meals out to celebrate birthdays, or wider family or the hope of children. It was all gone.

I tried to hold on to the prospect of eventual improvement, both in my circumstances and my emotional fragility – and of things somehow starting to feel less oriented around rootlessness and displacement. It was hard beyond measure to stay focused on the future. But here occasional forays into biblical texts were helpful, or at least not totally discomforting or without value. 'For everything there is a season', declaims the writer of Ecclesiastes, 'and a time for every matter under heaven':

'*A time to be born, and a time to die;*
A time to plant, and a time to pluck up what is planted..
A time to weep, and a time to laugh;
A time to mourn, and a time to dance ...
A time to seek, and a time to lose;
A time to keep, and a time to cast away.'[1]

Such texts were not so much beacons of hope as way-markers of forbearance; but they did at least hold out a sense that all human beings, both in the present and in the past, have had in their own difficult and highly particularised – but at the same time universal – ways to try to wrestle with and make sense of absence, even if solace or comfort may be nowhere within immediate reach. I attempted to think of fresh beginnings, of the possibility of finding new friendships, satisfactions, or even love, in unexpected places. Perhaps through endurance and sacrifice my boat could yet make it through the battered north way to welcoming harbours in different lands. And indeed I did finally climb out of that pit of despair; I did eventually find a handhold at the top of the crater, where light was shining down to the huddled figure at the bottom of the shaft, and haul myself onto the surface of a world I could recognise and understand and which understood me; and I did eventually meet someone new whom in the end I married in her home city in Italy. It felt during all this time that I had indeed gained some curious stature in waiting. Revival and transformation were not things that came easily or quickly or without many steps backward. The path towards the light was depressingly tough and uncertain. But the sense that I might not make it all, and doubt that there was anything worthwhile at the end of the road, turned out in the end to be a promising route. In mystery and ambiguity lay a horizon pregnant with possibility, even if at the time it was mostly occluded.

Our inescapable reality is that eventually we are all going to have to wrestle with loss. However insured

we feel, however barricaded against the intrusion of
calamity, we are utterly mistaken in that security. A
week after my marriage ended, my father rang me to
tell me he had cancer. I recall the precise moment of our
conversation because I had booked for a night into a small
hotel room in west London, whose walls were plastered
with wallpaper dominated by a startlingly vibrant pink
parrot. One salmon-coloured parrot would have been
unsettling enough; but here before me there were scores
of the wretched things. I remember with disagreeable
clarity my feelings of disjuncture and dismay in receiving
this horridly unwelcome news while simultaneously
being confronted by the plumage and feathers of a bird,
replicated nightmarishly across all four walls, that was
all puffed-up with a vulgar vitality that now seemed
obscene. In fact, it felt like an assault. Why should these
self-satisfied parakeets be so obviously pleased with
themselves, sitting pretty on their wallpapered branches,
when my poor dad was having to face up to the fact of his
imminent mortality? Somehow the blow of my father's
illness seemed bound up inseparably with the outrage
stirred by the massed and colourful parrots; and indeed
it all connected with my prior feelings of abandonment
and of things coming to an emotionally savage terminus.
These are the moments which shape us and make us
who we are – the moments which change everything and
which we also know we will never forget. For all their
brutality, they help us recognise that there are things we
can never control, over which we have no safe purchase.
Of course we do not want to relinquish those whom we
love, since to wish to hold on to the people and family
who mean so much to us is one of the more admirable
of human qualities. Cherishing others is what makes life
worth living. Yet perhaps to aspire to live forever, to have
what we cherish for all time, would be to acquire living
at the expense of life. To paraphrase Ursula Le Guin,
only that is properly and completely ours which we are
willing to lose.[2]

This does not make the fact of letting go any simpler or easier. We mourn for those we love, and we may never stop doing so. The same is true of the places we yearn for; from which we are now exiles. Tolkien and his fantastical Middle-earth are not to everyone's taste, and for some readers the *Weltanschauung* of *The Lord of the Rings* appears mawkish or lacking in depth of characterisation; but there is no doubt that he writes with considerable psychological insight into what it feels like to long for a loved land to which one can never again return – or at least only through arduous struggle and loss. The Eldar, or elves, of Middle-earth (approximate to the Midgard of Norse myth) are not native to the place at all. They are age-old migrants from the Undying Lands, far away to the West, and their sense of estrangement from and longing for their true homeland never really leaves them. As Paul Kocher puts it, 'The elves lose vital energy which can be replenished only in Valinor ... they are obeying the homing-impulse for Valinor deeply implanted in all their race'.[3] When Frodo and his companions rest for a while *en route* to the Prancing Pony at Bree and a rendezvous with the wizard Gandalf, and hunted as they are by the menacing Black Riders, the travellers fortuitously encounter in the wood a group of elves on their way out of Middle-earth. Uppermost in the minds of these wanderers is not the upcoming struggle with Sauron, deadly enemy of the free peoples, but rather their final departure across Belegaer, the Great Sea. They yearn to go back to Eldamar in the furthest West of the world. As Kocher puts it: 'Gildor and his band ... are feeling this homesickness when they meet the hobbits in the Shire woods. "We exiles," he tells them, "and most of our kindred have long ago departed, and we too are now only tarrying here a while, ere we return over the Great Sea." The lovely hymn these elves chant to Elbereth is full of nostalgia for the Undying Lands. They have lost interest in earthly affairs. Sauron is not in their thoughts'.[4] While Gildor *et al.* offer the hobbits protection for the night, they do so somewhat half-heartedly, or at least distractedly. Like political neutrals confronted by some looming totalitarian menace, they are simply not engaged by the great fight that is to come.

This narrative device of loss and exile enables Tolkien to portray the elves as fundamentally alien, as forever looking to further horizons. They might incidentally get involved in the sufferings and doings of others; but as a rule of thumb such matters are not really what they want to do or who they really want to be. The yearning for Valinor that they exhibit thus serves to make them seem somewhat otherworldly, as if their concerns for others are not quite earnest or deep. They are giving themselves up, in a sort of melancholy languor, to the exile's grand sensation of longing. The generic world-weariness of their race makes those individuals among the elves who *do* get involved in the affairs of Middle-earth seem that much more impressive. Arwen and Elrond, for example, do not depart from the world without at least considerable ambivalence. Kocher again: 'They leave Middle-earth with reluctance. Tolkien pictures them sitting together under the stars far into the night, looking to the chance wanderer like grey figures carved in stone, unspeaking, but in thought "recalling the ages that were gone and all their joys and labours in the world, or holding council, concerning the days to come". One wonders how content they will be in the Undying Lands. These are not Paradise. No beatific vision or new celestial life awaits the returning elves. In the endless tranquillity will Haldir and the others of Galadrim cease to long for the mallorn trees of Lorien of the Blossom, or Elrond for some struggle or other which he can lead?'.[5] In fact, like the longings for Ithaca of Odysseus, a return from exile may by no means be straightforward. The landscape of loss is fraught with ambiguity. We may all have our sea-longings; but while we have been out in the world, and attempted to change it, the world in its turn has altered us. We are no longer perhaps the people we were. We have revived. To wish to go back to what we were, or to the places we knew at a different time, is to hope for a planet that no longer exists. What matters is acknowledging and dealing with forfeiture. This might be a thoroughly difficult and unsettling, even upsetting, process. But a false nostalgia, a nostalgia into which we might throw ourselves as if into a languid and beautiful dream, is exactly that: a falsehood which overlooks the fact that the world changes all the time and we must change with it. Nothing lasts forever – neither wife, nor parents, nor home. Indeed, as Milan Kundera rightly realises, it is the very shortness and truncated pathos of our lives which makes nostalgia for homeland or loved landscape possible at all: 'If after 20 years abroad an émigré were to come back to his native land with another hundred years of life ahead of him, he would have little sense of a Great Return, for him it would probably not be a return at all, just one of many byways in the long journey of his life. For the very notion of homeland, with all its emotional power, is bound up with the relative brevity of our life, which allows us too little time to become attached to some other country, to other countries, to other languages'.[6]

In his affecting memoir of early adulthood in Sweden, the *Guardian*'s writer on religion Andrew Brown recounts life in his adopted country following marriage to a Swedish woman he met in the mid-seventies in North Wales. Writing articles in English for the British press, often about Swedish news stories, but speaking Swedish at home to spouse Anita and son Felix, Brown fly-fished in a lake near his home of Uddevalla and grew away from his wife. Eventually he moved to London and secured a bed-sit in a Bayswater mews, perhaps not too far in fact from my own later basement studio in the same neighbourhood. Like me, Brown felt himself to be an exile – but from where? Was he longing for a life in England, at the *Spectator*, where he could play at being a fake Englishman with a double life[7] in a city, London, that 'filled all horizons',[8] or for an isolate stretch of water in Sweden (whither for a while he returned) where he could fish in silence? The sense of displacement was considerable: 'I went back to Uddevalla to organise things with Anita', he writes, 'and we all went out to the lake house to camp for the last time. I don't think we ever quarrelled there. The pressure of other people's domesticity was too much. All our friends were divorced except us, and the lake house had become a sort of shrine for some of them: a place where they could build a house where people didn't quarrel and betray each other ... Afterwards, I walked down to the lake. I could see across the water a grove of birch trees and their reflections, all very empty, all very clear. It was still evening, almost as bright as daylight; but the sun had long gone and with it the warmth of the day, the air had a blue metallic tinge as if it had changed places with the lake. Nothing disturbed the water; not even the memory of yearning. For a long time I had been home in exile but now I couldn't get back.'[9] Neither properly of one place or of the other, Brown here correctly identifies the perennial burden of the expatriate: from wherever you are from, in whichever place you now find yourself, you can never return untransformed – however much you might ache for what you once knew, and feel alienated by your present context – to what you left behind. This is not because the landscape has changed (though change it might, and probably will). It is because you have. The place where you lived and loved is gone – not because it now exists in a different place, but because it lies unreachable in another time. You have become an outlaw to your own history and your past self.

My own sense of exile from the coast has helped me better to understand that not all homecomings can be happy ones. What we once had is lost. Nostalgia is indeed a longing for what can never come again. We may return, and sometimes it is good to do so, at least temporarily; but what we find on the abandoned shores may be very different from what we left behind. It is true that what we now are, the people we have become, is made up of the places we have been in the past and the rich experiences we have had there. Philip Toynbee, for one, understands well the pull and power of reminiscence, and indeed that our memories must be celebrated. Those whom we loved, and the landscapes we enjoyed alongside them, must not be forgotten – to do so would be to lose not only them but also an important part of ourselves. Toynbee is wise when he writes, '*Far Away and Long Ago*. How those phrases tear at the heart! And though I know very well that attention must be paid to the present time and place; that nostalgia can be sentimental and evasive; yet the present moment is nothing without all the earlier moments which it contains. This view of a snow valley would be nothing unless I had seen many other and very different views'.[10] What we experience now, in other words, is the amalgam and accumulated sum of what we experienced back then. None of us exists only from moment to moment, without drawing on some essential bedrock of times past. The past and the sufferings and joys we are bound to endure there constitute our seedbed – what Rilke in his Tenth Duino Elegy called 'our winter-enduring foliage, our dark evergreen ... place and settlement, foundation and soil and home'.[11] Nevertheless, for all that that is true, the proper place of the exile is indeed elsewhere. A false clinging to the landscape of loss will result only in an irresolvable sadness, a closed inwardness and unwillingness further to develop the self. None of us wants to ossify. We owe it to ourselves as human beings to embrace the future and the mystery and challenge of living, however doubtful and uncertain we may be about what the future holds.

The poet Charles Tomlinson, one of the most sensitive of modern landscape writers, addresses with characteristic economy and elegance the sense of dislocation induced by exile in his poem 'Far Point'. Deep in the Canadian wilderness, with mountains and conifers rising up on all sides, this is a place which feels like the end of the world:

'The road ends here. If your way
lies north, then you must take
to the forest or the bay. A café
which is a poolroom which is a bar
serves clams and beer;
the woman who brings them in,
a cheerful exile here,
counts out coins
'Eins, zwei, drei...'
with the queen's head on them.'[12]

Places which feel like endings, or the closing of a chapter, may actually offer new beginnings – whether they involve cheerfully handling the currency of a new, adopted nation in the context of some isolated way-station, or leaving your place of origin to embrace some other aspect of challenging life or landscape. And, as Tomlinson implies, there is invariably some sense of transcendence to be found, to be excavated from the rock-face, most particularly in a topography that reveals its hidden glories slowly: which rewards patience, and whose clouds of unknowing may actually be the inspiring summits of slowly materialising peaks, rising upwards and upwards as if towards the creator himself:

'Across the blue-grey strait,
the ragged ideograms of firs
in a rising and falling fog:
clouds are what we appear to contemplate
above them, then the mist
stirs, sails off
and we see it is summits
we are peering at,
that go on unveiling themselves
as if they were being created.'[13]

Whether lived here, or there, our short and troubled lives are circled by doubts that we as individuals are making any difference at all in the great mass of humanity and over the long centuries of human history. But it is precisely such incertitude over our significance which makes us human and which makes our humanity valuable. It is because we know that we have to give things up, to leave them, that enables others to take our place in the great drama of birth, life and death. In deference to the process of entropy, as John Bowker makes clear, life has to yield to life for life to happen at all.[14] Or as Frodo says to his friend Sam Gamgee, whom he loves and whom he must leave in order to be healed elsewhere of the pains and wounds garnered as Ringbearer: 'I tried to save the Shire, and it has been saved, but not for me. It must often be so, Sam, when things are in danger: someone has to give them up, lose them, so that others may keep them'.[15] It is precisely the business of loss – and of our corresponding doubts that we are making anything worthwhile of our lives – that renders our struggles in the world intrinsically worthwhile.

The business of living inevitably involves sacrifice, of letting go, and it is often a sacrifice that tears at the heart. When we stand at the Grey Havens, wherever that may be, and see our dear companions take ship for the last time on earth, they do so finally and forever. There is no coming back from the shores of this world. This is the last farewell here on earth. We do not know where we have come from, or where we are going. The challenge of such absoluteness can lead to different solutions and responses. For the atheist, there may be dignity to be mined from the mere facts of human biological existence – of evolution and adaptation in the context of a ceaselessly changing and implacable universe. While for the believer, sacred scripture and tradition appear to offer a route to an eventual supersession of corporeal life in this world and transition to another plane or mode of being. Neither position, despite what their differing advocates might claim, offers anything other than complete uncertainty. There are no – and there never have been – definitive answers to the most enigmatic and unfathomable question that there is: why are we here? It is precisely in that very uncertainty that I believe the true worth of our humanity can be found. My own sympathies, as will be evident from what has come before, lie much more with a religious view of the world than with atheism (in common with most people in Britain, at least according to the statistics).[16] But what these sympathies amount to – what I might call a 'sensibility of hope' – have been tested sorely by my shattering and unexpected divorce, the illness of both my parents and disorienting removal from one part of the country to another. Nevertheless, I would still want to argue – even in the face of the stark adversity that can pulverise all stability – that it is precisely in the fact that nothing *is* certain, *or* to be relied on, that we begin to understand the true workings of the world and of our place within it. And furthermore, that such agnosticism may have transcendent meaning and value.

The travel writer Rory MacLean (who coincidentally shares my mother's maiden name, albeit with a variant spelling) exemplifies just such defiant agnosticism in the subject matter of his inspiring book *Falling for Icarus*. Following the illness and death from cancer of his mother, MacLean resolved to go to Crete to build a flying machine. This was not to satisfy some suppressed or latent desire to become an aviator. It was rather about a longing to experience transcendence, to rise above the mud and dirt of the world and the grief brought on by mortality and loss. In MacLean's own words, 'I hadn't set out to become a pilot. I'd simply set my heart on lifting off the ground in an attempt to lighten my despair. I'd wanted to bid farewell to my mother and to recognise the power of love and life to transform sadness. Then, with a ritual dip of my wings, I'd wanted to come back down to earth'.[17] MacLean wondered if in the course of building his flying machine, firing the engine, rising towards the empyrean and ducking and weaving through dangerous air currents, he might receive some sign from his dead parent, some moment of grace or beatification: 'In the few seconds of my flight, suspended between earth and sky, I'd half-hoped to hear my mother's voice. I'd imagined her flying alongside me saying, "Well done, darling, but do keep your nose down." I had wanted to tell her the story of the Woodhopper and our time in Annisari, its tall tales and hot, wine-soaked days. I'd hoped to say that I missed her. Of course, I'd heard nothing above the buzz of the engine for there was nothing to hear. No voice had called me from the silent dust. Instead my solitary flight, and the good fortune of my survival, encouraged me to a new life'.[18] Reason and logic are here held in poignant tension with hope. MacLean knew in fact that he would hear no consoling sound, have no actual moment of contact from beyond; but he hoped and expected nevertheless that in aspiring for lift, for flight – in making a bold actual and symbolic leap towards the heavens – he would yet receive something approximating to transcendent meaning and value. Such an attitude might seem naïve or foolish to those who simply want to rationalise the mysteries of a universe we can never hope at bottom fully to understand. For those to whom not only all truth, but all explanation, is held at the bottom of a microscope, and for whom meaning is measured solely by empirical facts, MacLean's hopeful agnosticism can only seem self-deluding, albeit, in the circumstances of loss, understandable. I like to think however that it represents something else – something more than simply a self-indulgent but ultimately false and futile longing.

To try to grasp a sense of transcendent meaning, however fleeting, Rory MacLean went to 'elemental Crete', as he describes it – the island from which Icarus took flight with Daedalus, and the island 'where the Minoans had reached out to catch the essence of the passing moment, among a people with a raw, unpredictable, admirable energy for life'.[19] Other than north Norfolk, the place of my own that is perhaps most connected or associated with a transcendent sensibility is Italy, a nation famed – just as Greece is – for its zest for living. I first travelled there in the mid-1980s, on various school and pre-university trips where I was fortunate enough to be introduced to the overwhelming artistic and cultural riches of that epicentre of the Renaissance. The most memorable of those visits was in the company of a group of young people similarly interested in art history, many of whom later became close friends (more than thirty years later I remain in touch with some of them). The wonders of Venice, Rome, Florence and Siena that unfolded on that visit brought home to me just how powerful and impressive the religious impulse has been in the creation of stupendous artwork, buildings and sculpture. And this too seems to be an element missing from Dawkins' flamboyant denunciations of religion. Yes, the imperative towards belief can be twisted and exploited for malign ends, just as the rationalistic or scientific impulse may similarly be perverted by those who want to misuse knowledge in the abuse and pursuit of power. There are *of course* plenty of people in the world who claim religiosity and who drape their warped and repellent ideals in the flag of faith. But the sheer beauty of artefacts inspired by a religious sensibility should give us pause for thought. There is something good and truthful in the manifestation of the beautiful when it celebrates something that lies beyond the self-interest or self-absorption of human beings. There may be no transcendent being, but it is hard not to feel otherwise when walking between the echoing black and white marbled pillars of Siena's Gothic cathedral or contemplating Titian's exquisite altarpiece, 'The Assumption of the Virgin', in the soaring Frari church of Venice.[20] Indeed, it is precisely in the creation and appreciation of art that Keith Ward detects what he calls the capacity for 'spiritual perception.'[21] It's perfectly true of course that the motivation of our talented ancestors for glorifying the idea of God in paint and marble and stone does not add up to proof of existence. Though, as Philip Toynbee suggests, it is also true 'that the need is no *proof* that God exists; but it is at least a suggestive and interesting element in many people's composition. Strange creatures, if we felt so strong a need for something which was never there'.[22]

In his 'Italian' novel *Sandro and Simonetta*, published in 1992, Richard Burns records the doomed love of the painter Sandro Filipepi, nicknamed Botticelli, for the beautiful Simonetta Vespucci amidst the teeming and often violent backstreets of fifteenth-century Florence. Struck down by illness, Simonetta, immortalised by Botticelli in his painting 'The Birth of Venus'[23] dies young, leaving the painter utterly bereft and nursing an angry grief 'brimming with the awareness of all that might have been and never was.'[24] Yet despite the agony and the sorrow he is left with, and his sense of cruel abandonment by lover and fate, Sandro finds himself still able to reflect thus on the nature of memory, the past and artistic creation: 'History is not what is lost but what remains, not what has vanished but what survives', he says. 'The rest, the spaces between the records and the artefacts, we fill with conjecture, illuminate with connection. The patterns we make of the past are like the patterns I make with my paints, showing not reality as it is or was but rather reality as perceived ... I cannot see with God's eye, see the wholeness, the entirety of eternity. I am the fly on the canvas, skirting the pennon and the woman's foot. Yet I am also human, and therefore touched with the divine, albeit in corrupt and adulterated form, so I still try to make my patterns, still try to make my five senses make sense. My life is an arrow's flight, a trajectory, an arc that will end in my death; my life is my city's life – growth, splendour and decay. And the history through which I move, that too can be granted design and shape, as though, touched with the divine, I can grasp the edge of the divine pattern.'[25] These words might have been written not just as a eulogy for Sandro Botticelli, or even for all those who reflect with sadness on loss and the uncertainty of what happens next, but also for the novelist himself. Richard Burns, one of the most brilliant talents of his generation, took his own life one day before his thirty-fourth birthday.[26] Like the Simonetta Vespucci about whom he wrote, he too died very young. He never got to see his own novel in print. Yet for all that he may have been tortured by demons during his lifetime, for all that depression ate away at his own sense of self,[27] what he has left behind him is a profound meditation on the nature of art, and of the continuing capacity of literary and artistic creation to move and transport us even after the passing of its creator. The troubled and tragic Burns, just like his character Botticelli, was touched not just by star quality but perhaps even by divinity. What truly matters in life is the patterning we make with the paints at our disposal. The patterns may not make much sense at the time, which is the nature of living a life that is inevitably, and throughout, characterised by doubt as to what it means and where it is heading. But looked at from above, from a God's-eye view, the result may yet be meaningful. As Sandro says at the end of this remarkable and beautiful novel: 'When I painted, when I touched the panel with my brush and made a world of pigment, perhaps then I knew a special truth ... The truth is not measurable in inches and miles. The truth is the whole of it, not just what we see but what we make of what we see. If you seek the truth of my life look not to my words but my pictures.'[28]

Burns issues a salutary reminder of the significance of what is left, not what is gone. An endless pull towards the past may indeed be a siren's call. However, returning to northern Italy to get married for a second time inevitably did involve my immersion in a kind of nostalgia. In walking the streets of Padua with my new wife, and then spending time in Florence for our honeymoon, I did see a succession of ghosts in the *piazze* and the *trattorie* and the *negozi*. Confronted again by the welcome sight of the antique Hotel Porta Rossa, the unchanged albergo where I had stayed with friends thirty years before, I did mourn the loss of youth and of past avenues now long travelled: of the young man just starting out in life with all his roads and choices ahead of him. Battered by time and circumstance, even if buoyed up by new love, I now felt much older and much wearier. There is no question that a second marriage always involves uncertainty because of what has been experienced beforehand. You cannot approach such a serious commitment without bearing scars, or without a sense that all such decisions are a huge risk. But these doubts are not only important, they are essential. It is only through such agnosticism about what the future holds that we are able to move forward with any degree of integrity or authenticity at all. We don't know what's around the corner; and any certainty or misbelief that we can control our destiny in that respect is a mistaken one. But through a combination of good fortune and fortitude we can still get somewhere worth getting to. This surely is the way out of the pit with its distant patch of light at the top, or of the dark cell wherein we feel trapped without hope of release. Ursula Le Guin writes that 'outside the locked room is the landscape of time, in which the spirit may, with luck and courage, construct the fragile, makeshift, improbable roads and cities of fidelity: a landscape inhabitable by human beings'.[29] An endless pining for a landscape that has ossified, that has passed into memory as something unchanging – frozen in time in its melancholy and lost perfection – is a chimera, a mirage and a false dream. However, to be part of a landscape that one knows and loves from of old, and which changes as one changes with it, is perhaps a different matter. This is the topography of revival and rebirth: not just the Veneto of Giotto or of a youth looking to the future but that of man in early middle age whose future has arrived even as he enjoys and celebrates the past. As Le Guin rightly reflects 'It is not until an act occurs within the landscape of past and future that it is a human act. Loyalty, which asserts the continuity of past and future, binding time into a whole, is the root of human strength; there is no good to be done without it'.[30] Past and future may then indeed be reconciled by a questioning, optimistic faith in the possibility of something better: the result of an agnostic, but open-minded, sensibility of hope. Moving forwards is, then, the most and the least that we can do.

What then is my own next chapter? My home is now in Oxford, and I visit Norfolk only occasionally. The sense of loss – not just of the landscape itself but of everything that it means and is bound up with – will probably never leave me. I know that in my emotional DNA it comprises a time and a place that will always be profoundly important. But in acknowledging that fact I recognise, too, that to try to hold onto it as it was would be self-defeating. That time, and the place that existed during that time, are finished. The good things that have come to me since would not have come to pass had I remained in what Le Guin rightly calls the locked room. It is only outside of that room, however sceptical or uncertain one may be about the future, that we can move forward into a space and a landscape where we can again try to be believing human beings – believing, that is, in a future in which we can once more play a positive part, as active participants rather than as those to whom things have happened or been done. It is the attempt not to try to control things, but to make sense of your past and future in fresh ways, that is important. And that does involve letting go of certainty.

In her novel *Moon Tiger*, a deserving winner of the Booker Prize in 1987, Penelope Lively writes wisely and movingly of the agonising loss involved in love and war. Claudia Hampton, a popular historian living in Cairo is posted to the front as a war reporter. There she falls in love with a young tank officer, Tom Southern, who is killed in the western desert during the confused and uncertain Allied push against Rommel. Looking back on her life from a distance of forty years hence, Claudia believes that her doomed relationship with Tom was the centre and fulcrum of her existence. What has happened since is perhaps only commentary – an epilogue. But when Tom is killed, she has to move on. It is imperative. She realises that to create a shrine in her heart for her lost lover, and spend all her remaining time on this earth tending and contemplating it, would lead to a life characterised only by an endless, sterile middle. Addressing the dead Tom from her own deathbed, Claudia offers the following reflection: 'You are young; I am old. You are in some ways unreachable, shut away behind a glass screen of time; you know nothing of forty years of history and forty years of my life; you seem innocent, like a person in another century. But you are also, now, a part of me, as immediate and as close as my own other selves, all the Claudias of whom I am composed'.[31] Tom will forever be part of who Claudia is – even as she knows that, had he lived, so much of her life would have been richer and more complete. Yet final separation is not the end: 'Death is total absence, you said. Yes and no. You are not absent so long as you are in my head … It might be easier if I believed in God, but I don't. All I can think, when I hear your voice, is that the past is true, which both appals and uplifts me. I need it; I need you … Because unless I am part of everything I am nothing.'[32]

The loss of that which we love can be brutal. Richard Burns and Penelope Lively, remarkable novelists both, understand that truth profoundly. But in order to revive and live again we all have to embrace that loss. The resurrection involved may or may not be a religious one. It may be characterised by as many steps backward as uncertain moves forward. Incertitude will never be far away. As Claudia says, it would be easier to embrace religious belief to help her make sense of her life, but she does not. Yet in her hopeful, agnostic impulse to embrace the treasured past in order to make better sense of the future, and move ahead, she is incarnating in her life a sense of the transcendent that is both meaningful and valid. Landscapes of doubt, however littered they may be with the broken shells of old boats, may also theatres of hope. Through the fog, and beyond the sea-frets that chill you to the bone, there may yet be a way out of the marshes to the unknown uplands.

CONCLUSION

RETURN

Breckland: one of the least familiar topographies of England. Home to heath and butterfly and yellow gorse: once domesticated, now running wild again. It is here that flint was extracted by those inventive Neolithic miners at Grimes Graves – and here too that the landscape was pockmarked by post-glacial pingos: ancient ponds scattered across the upland like the copious teardrops of some lost and wandering giant. It is as if Gog and his brother Magog lumbered through here, grieving, before they halted on the summits of the downs named after them in nearby Cambridgeshire. This is a moorland hidden away, resonant with secrecy, sparsely populated – but only superficially unremarkable. Undulating plain of anonymity, it is a site of veneration that rewards greater scrutiny than it receives. In Thompson village, heart of the Brecks, a farmhouse conceals the panelled walls of a lost medieval college. In 1349 a master and five chaplains were installed here by an aristocratic family to recite prayers for the souls of their parents in the nearby chantry of St Martin's Church. This was no dry, academic spirituality, but instead the passionate faith of a *beleaguered community in bondage to the Plague. Their prayers were pleas: not in celebration of some remote or abstract deity, but rather to hold fear of death at bay. These people doubted they would survive. I come back still to Thompson, just as I came before with her. I return to listen to the silence, and wander between those enigmatic and prehistoric ponds, heavy-laden at times with summer dragonflies, to reflect on priests who turned earnestly to God not knowing or believing if tomorrow they would walk the sunlit earth.*

Stripped back to the bone, bare of foliage since mid-November, the spidery branches of Norfolk's winter trees extend their probing fingers towards a rapidly darkening west. Away to my right, in the chill and gathering twilight, Cley windmill looms out of the shadows like a stolid and brooding colossus, incongruously bedecked with fairy lights as its stationary sails – frozen in overhanging space, an incongruous Norfolk saltire – rise suspended above me as if in homage to a painting by Vermeer. No Delft, this, but rather the neighbouring coastline of eastern England, whose susurrating reedbeds stretch away in front of me in a maze of channels, runnels and hidden tributaries. The wind, as it sprints along the foreshore, seems to be speaking only to me, imparting some obscure but vital message. It is then, with the report of a gunshot, that a great moving skein rises clattering and screaming from the nearby hills of Blakeney, whose church is inkily outlined on a horizon now fizzing and spitting in affront – defiant last stand of crimsons and golds – while, covert as a thief, evening steals the day away. An army of pink-footed geese rises ethereally above the desiccated moorings of the former Glaven Ports, passing in massed and irregular formation overhead, as if in retreat from this final dying of the light. They are returning now to their breeding grounds in Iceland. Alongside their black-bellied brent cousins, fated to fly forever between transitory coast and their anchorage in

arctic Russia, these pink-feet have no permanent home.
Migrants of time and tides, they are visitors in transit.
Weekend guest myself, hasty sad revenant to this seascape
of lost hopes, I too exist between spaces and places. My
heart may belong to Norfolk; yet it beats and functions
and loves elsewhere.

'I strove towards thee, and was repulsed by thee that I
might taste death. The disturbed and darkened vision of
my mind was being healed from day to day by the keen
salve of wholesome pains. I became wretched, and thou
nearer.'
– **St Augustine**

'Thou hast given me on earth this godlike soul,
And a poor prisoner of it thou has made
Behind flesh-walls; from that wretched state
How can I rescue it, how my true life find?
All goodness, Lord, must fail without thy aid:
For thou alone hast power to alter fate.'
– **Michelangelo**

'He it is that desireth in thee, and He it is that is desired.'
– **Walter Hilton**

In this short book I have attempted to reflect, in ways
that I hope some might find helpful, on the worth and
value of uncertainty. In so doing I have used some of my
own experiences, particularly in relation to the failure of
my former marriage and my sense of exile from a loved
home elsewhere, to try to put concrete flesh on the more
abstract bones of discussion about belief and its opposite.
It is not about the marriage or the topography of home
as such: those are the backdrops, the supporting scenery

if you like, to what I have wanted to say about the false hopes offered by conviction and by the sense of security that arises from thinking that in life you can have access to all the answers. In fact, as I have tried to convey – against the assurances espoused alike by atheists and utterly convinced believers – we don't as human beings have very many answers at all to the universe's mysteries and challenges. Like a shifting runnel of water on Holkham Beach, life is an elusive and meandering conundrum, and all our confidences can be unpicked as quickly as a delicate spider's web in a rain shower. We live in houses of sand, whose very foundations – just like the changing strandline and contours of the Norfolk coast – may slide and be displaced from moment to moment.

It is nevertheless a very human reaction to want to hold on to certainty. The very fragility of mortality, the nature of the frighteningly unstable ground around us, pushes us towards reaching for a handhold that might help us find a way through the challenging marshlands with which all of us, throughout our lives, are going to be confronted. It is proper and laudable to cherish family and friends, even if losing that which we love is actually the consequence of being alive. But while individual loss may be appalling – the loss of those closest to us, the things which we feel have made us most secure in our terrible fantasy of invulnerability, whether marriage, or job, or some other satisfaction – it is not always or necessarily the end. In honest doubt about where we are heading, in the fertile seedbed of agnosticism and in the hope of new life in fresh beginnings, there may still be found reasons to endure and to anticipate things changing for the better. I would argue, in fact, for an appreciation of the theological value to be found precisely in endurance, in incertitude and in the fact that much of the time we feel we are stumbling around in the mist with our compass needle pointing in the wrong direction. As W. H. Vanstone rightly says, waiting – even if the waiting often seems hopeless – always involves caring, or being involved: 'A person to whom few things are important rarely waits. A person who views the world with indifference rarely finds himself waiting. Conversely a person to whom many things matter will often find himself waiting. The experience of waiting is the experience of the world as in some sense *mattering*, as being of some kind of importance.'[1] For the world to matter, in the sense that Vanstone understands it, we have to accept that things don't always or even often go our way. That is the bargain of life and the condition of mortality. But we owe it to ourselves as human beings to hope that they might, even if that eventuality looks so far away as to be a tiny chink of light at the top of the pit of captivity.

A theology of hopeful anticipation recognises value above all in hiddenness, in concealment. It is an agnostic theology which recognises that creeds and dogmatic assertions often turn mystery and myth into a set of factual propositions which counterproductively evacuate the most moving stories of religious rebirth of their very capacity to transport us. Similarly, in our increasing dependence on technology and on the interconnection through social media that is no true connectedness, and in the distraction provided by the obvious and the shallow and the ephemeral – in that, in fact, which can be easily discarded rather than reflected upon, savoured or wondered at over time – we have in important respects turned our collective face in the West away from that which is real, and durable and beautiful. Whether the over-confident and insular credo of a theological systematics that cannot think beyond its own narrow strictures, the madness of religious fanaticism or the false bombast of atheistic assertion that finds meaning only in what can be cultivated in a petri dish: all are false gospels and severely limited and restricted in what they can offer. In order to be truly alive to the wonders the universe can contain, we need to reclaim the meaning of that which cannot be counted or measured or defined by either scripture or science. Only in losing ourselves in the sea-fret may we actually be able to find what we are looking for. The medieval mystics, as we have seen, understood this well. In looking for the light, they found transformative darkness; in not-seeing, a kind of seeing; and in the cloud of unknowing, a capacity for inner transformation wherein was contained all of the world's wisdom. In their very doubt and scepticism that they could reach God at all, they left behind a legacy comprising some of the most searching and profound of Christian religious literature.

Perhaps only in immersing ourselves in the darkness, in a preparedness to enter the pit – to experience desolation, deprivation and the loss of all hope – may we fully experience the light that blinds us when our release is eventually secured. Without knowing how black the blackness was, we would have no true conception of the nature of the light or of its capacity to drive darkness away. The same is true of faith. The great mystics would have had no real capacity to enter imaginatively into the sufferings and passion of Christ had they not also experienced an incapacity at times to sense his presence. By this reckoning, doubt is not something separate from faith, but is actually essential to it. The two are integral, indissoluble. It is thoroughly regrettable that, in the course particularly of Christian history, doubt has received so little acknowledgement or appreciation as the essential incubator of the lively and robust belief that may flourish in its care. It is in the experience of dereliction and abandonment that we come to a sense that we may not in the end have been finally abandoned. It is in the failure and retreat of love that we realise how precious a thing it is, and that we want to be able to experience it again. It is when we cry out to the unseen and unfelt heavens in full knowledge that perhaps only absence is staring back at us – and that all we hear is an echo – that we begin to understand the beginnings of the possibility that absence may actually be presence. It is here that metaphor and simile come to our rescue. The God of the New Atheists (or at least the God they wish to annihilate), as much as the God of some believing philosophers of religion, is so often religiously and philosophically impoverished:[2] stripped of the active, restless, searching energy of the medievals, and reduced to a 'big person' sitting on a cloud. God has thus been domesticated, conceived only in worldly or anthropomorphised terms. The worst consequences of such appropriation are to be seen in the lunatic delusions of the jihadis, for whom God is only properly God if he is on your side and committed to the destruction of those perceived not to believe what you do. The reality is that human language, of whatever kind (English, Arabic or some other vernacular) inevitably eviscerates the divine, which is why the best kind of theology has always been allusive, elliptical and analogical. It is a theology that seeks God not only in scriptural assertion but in poetry and language and music. As George Steiner rightly says, 'The limits of our language are not, *pace* Wittgenstein, those of our world … The arts are most wonderfully rooted in substance, in the human body, in stone, in pigment, in the twanging of gut or the weight of wind on reeds. All good art and literature begin in immanence. But they do not stop there. Which is to say, very plainly, that it is the enterprise and privilege of the aesthetic to quicken into lit presence the continuum between temporality and eternity, between matter and spirit, between man and 'the other'.[3] It is thus in the unsayable relationship of the hand with the bow or harp, of the lips with the oboe's reed, or in the inspiration of the artist as she or he brings a painting to wonderful completion, that we feel most keenly the movement of that which may actually be divine.

Any acknowledgement that the presence of God may be discernible to us only indirectly, never (as Job eventually saw him) face to face, might lead us to question whether theology has any value at all: an uncomfortable question for a theologian. Indeed, if God cannot be spoken about except analogically, or in terms of logical opposites, in fact of what he is not, then theology itself – literally 'talk about God' – might be rendered a highly questionable, if not actually meaningless, activity. But it is the right and proper task of those who think about absolutes to try – however falteringly or inadequately – to articulate the indeterminate and absolute in terms that approximate to what they are trying to communicate and conceptualise. What theologians should not I think attempt to do is reduce or corral the unsayable into a set of rigid factual propositions. As Philip Toynbee reminds us, 'It's wise to recognise that theology is not about God but about Man (sic) seeking for God; Heaven guessed at from earth'.[4] It is in exactly that process of *guessing* that doubt becomes a valuable motor in seeking an authentic way of determining where divinity might, at least roughly, be located. The story of God in the West is ultimately a story of paradox. It is the story of a timeless being who earnestly desires to be at one with a broken planet of his own making, and to communicate with the mortal, fallen creatures which inhabit it. The drama reaches its improbable apotheosis in the story of the Christian God who became man in the fragile and broken form of Jesus of Nazareth, executed by the Romans in a shameful criminal's death. This is a story that makes little sense unless and until you appreciate that all of existence is likewise paradoxical: we live out our small lives only to die; we love only to be disappointed by loss; we create never to see our creations outlast or outlive us. The whole of life is thus founded on a kind of perpetual negativity, on the premise that what we have can never permanently be held. It is thus in negativity itself, in the absence that – precisely because we have to endure impermanence and get on with the business of living – is also a sort of presence, that we are able to recognise both ourselves and sometimes also the premise and possibility of external divinity. Doubt is an utterly appropriate heuristic for such speculation because only dubiety can make sense of the imponderable, or chimes with the way that people have no meaningful control over their existence or the direction in which they are heading.

The capacity to doubt also implies the capacity to believe, just as the capacity to believe suggests the capacity to question. Doubt and faith do not cancel one another out. They are not mutually toxic. They are both part of a mature and appropriately interrogatory perspective on the world and of our place within it. The coastline may crumble; our lives and our loves may be swept into the voracious sea; but marram grass continues to sway evocatively on the dune. Even on the windswept sands, where wilderness runs away on all sides, pinkish-lilac sea-lavender – together with the leafy spikes of sea-wormwood and the blue, umbel-like clusters of sea-aster – can be found if you seek them out in cheerful hope and with sufficient determination. Meanwhile, in the cool and shady pinewoods adjacent to the enigmatic foreshore may be seen the lovely bell-shaped flowers of the harebell; while further inland are sweet-briar, wood-sorrel, marsh-sorrel, dog-rose and St John's wort, this last beloved of those who seek remedy for depression and melancholia. We may feel we have lost the lands and people we have loved, we may feel forever exiled from them, but our capacity for endurance – of the perennial flowering of life on the very edge of desolation, once the storm has passed – should never be dismissed or underestimated. When I lost my home, and my wife, I thought that they were truly lost. But north Norfolk endures, and I am married again. It is right to celebrate that which we had, and to acknowledge that the places and spaces which we loved have made us the people that we are. To paraphrase Tennyson, we are a part of all that we have met. Yet at the same time, as the poet rightly says, all experience is an archway through which gleams a bright and untraversed world, rich in both possibility and promise. The sense of exile is always relative. It may also, as Milan Kundera reminds us, turn into a false and clinging nostalgia that is no true reflection of what it evokes. To adhere to an idea of what was, and then turn it in effect into an idol that encompasses everything thought to be fundamentally valuable or significant, is to betray both ourselves and our capacity for recovery – as well as the past itself. The past is indeed and altogether another country; and what people do there is probably not at all what we thought they did, either then or now.

These landscapes of the past, as much as the physical geography of a relinquished and much loved homeland, are the settings not only of perennial forfeiture and renewal but also the maps of our own hearts with all their varied and passionate longings. Criss-crossed as they are by the dykes and watercourses that serve as junctions and way-markers for our journey through life, the varied features – all the bumps, tumuli and unexpected undulations – of these landscapes are the marks and scars that have been carved into our unique emotional histories by the passage from one sandy dune to another. The meaning of our lives may be right there in the charts; but sometimes – as the filmmaker Vincent Ward astutely reminds us – all they tell you is that you are lost.[5] We have to remember, in the midst of profound uncertainty, that however far from familiar banks we may wander, however buffeting the water in the centre of the river, it is not necessarily the end of things to wade out into cloying mud or stumble around for a while in the uncharted backlands. Indeed, to have to surrender one terrain may actually be to take possession, however fleetingly, of another. When I go back now to Norfolk in the autumn I take delight in the thousands of migratory birds that likewise return to roost in the marsh, salt and reedbeds. Pink-footed, brent and white-footed geese can be seen here in such numbers that their total absence in the spring seems so unlikely as to be almost inconceivable. Yet within months they will be gone, flown away to their arctic breeding grounds, and the countryside that was their habitat will again be an

abandoned landscape of loss. I recognise now that there
is no single resting place either for them or for me;
like mine, their home is both here and there. They are
migratory creatures who exist on the winds, on the bright
and violent ether through which they soar from season
to season. Their movements are ambivalent; they are not
of any single place, yet equally comfortable in several.
They are both present and absent, just as we might think
of God. It is in terms of a similar kind of ambiguity that
we might profitably reflect on the Breckland priests of
College Farm, living and worshipping and finally dying
in fourteenth-century Thompson. Though imbued with
a medieval faith that was perhaps robust, they must
naturally have doubted, even as the Black Death raged
around them while scything down neighbours and
friends, if they would survive to recite next day's prayer
in the chantry. It was in recognition of such temporality
and mortality - of their own limited and troubled time
on this earth - that they were able to conceive and make
sense of the eternal in the context of whatever truncated
life might be left to them. It was in the immanent and
ambivalent that the capacity for belief was able to take
shape. The landscape they have left is yet haunted -
even in absentia - by their presence, in the stillness and
drowsy heaviness of the nearby kettle ponds, in the
resonant atmosphere of the former college itself. This is
a topography in which the eternal has left its footprint:
it is a place in which you can find yourself, however
transitory that person may be.

In *Exploring Doubt* I have made a plea for the value of
mystery, of the value of what is unknown to us as much as
what is known. I have argued that just as the New Atheists
have missed the point, so too have the religious literalists.
I have tried to suggest that throughout Christian
tradition some of the most fertile minds have made sense
of their beliefs fundamentally through the exploration of
doubt and - especially via rich and enigmatic metaphors
of ascent, interiority and darkness - ambiguity. My hope

is that this short work might encourage others to give honest dubiety its proper due; for it is surely in incertitude that we become most properly and completely ourselves and thus open to the possibility of transformation, even in the face of our ending. I think often, in this regard, of the moving valediction by Katharine Clifton[6] in the late Anthony Minghella's fine film adaptation of Michael Ondaatje's novel *The English Patient*: perhaps one of the most defiant instances of the articulation of hope in the face of ultimate uncertainty. In its simplicity and candour it strips human aspiration down to the bone, to its bare fundamentals. Following a plane crash in wartime Libya, László de Almásy, the eponymous patient of the film's title, is compelled to leave the badly injured Katharine behind in a remote cave while he seeks rescue across the burnt and burning Sahara sands: that is, alone, with diminishing water and food, and eventually no light. In those pregnant final hours before her battery is exhausted, Katharine finds herself able to marvel once again at a brilliant find of Neolithic rock paintings (astonishingly revealed after countless centuries, and discovered on a Royal Geographical Society mapping survey and archaeological expedition earlier in the film by Almásy and his British companion Peter Madox) which depict human swimmers;[7] their lithe and sinuous forms advance hauntingly and implausibly across the cave walls under the flickering light of her torch. Ten thousand years ago, we realise, this landlocked cave was close to an abundance of water. The passing of millennia – the waxing and waning of innumerable moons – has changed the face of the world. Rivers and lakes are now desert; the ancient swimmers, for all that they briefly move again, have been dead and gone for an eternity; all that remains is the memory and image of what once was. Yet for all that life seems lost, despite the fast approach of her own death, Katharine has the courage to continue writing 'in the darkness': to offer a last testament to the indestructibility of the human spirit, which in this instance yearns to be borne away to a 'Palace of Winds':

> '*My darling. I'm waiting for you. How long is the day in the dark? Or a week? The fire is gone, and I'm horribly cold. I really should drag myself outside but then there'd be the sun. I'm afraid I waste the light on the paintings, not writing these words. We die. We die rich with lovers and tribes, tastes we have swallowed, bodies we've entered and swum up like rivers. Fears we've hidden in – like this wretched cave. I want all this marked on my body. Where the real countries are. Not boundaries drawn on maps with the names of powerful men. I know you'll come carry me out to the Palace of Winds. That's what I've wanted: to walk in such a place with you. With friends, on an earth without maps. The lamp has gone out and I'm writing in the darkness.*'[8]

If sacred worth and meaning are to be found in migrating birds which fly north and south, east and west, or in the hope – however unlikely or infinitesimal – of eventual reunion with those we have loved, or in the capacity to begin life anew, then it is the very doubt and ambiguity of such hopes which render them meaningful. Whether in dust or in darkness, the transcendent value of writing of the dark as well as of the light – of doubt, not of proof or certainty – is surely worth celebrating, even if it means acknowledging the full loss of that which we love and have loved beyond measure.

NOTES

Preface and Acknowledgements

1   Peter Hitchens, *The Rage Against God*, p. 31.

Introduction: Arrival

1   See Jonathan Hooton, *The Glaven Ports*, p. 19: 'Older inhabitants remember heavy iron rings (now disappeared), set into the churchyard wall, which could only have been mooring rings'.

2   Ibid., p. 21.

3   Ibid., p. 19: 'The site of Cley haven is south of the major part of the present day village. The position of this inlet is still marked today by the triangular piece of grass known as Newgate Green, just south of the church. This area would have flooded at high tide and the roads that fork near the church and skirt either side of the green are where the vessels would have been pulled on shore. The site of the church beside Newgate Green is another indicator that this was the old centre of the village. It was not until after a major fire at the beginning of the seventeenth century that the village migrated further north, towards the sea. There are still a few houses lining the green at the foot of the magnificent church, to mark the former site of the medieval port of Cley.'

4   Milan Kundera, *Ignorance*, p. 34.

5   See also 'Face to faith', *Guardian*, 23 October 2010: 'Early frescoes in a Norfolk village remind us of our medieval churches' lively past, says Alex Wright'.

6   See Francis Pryor, *Seahenge*, p. 251: '"Seahenge" was never at sea. The timbers were constructed on dry land. Of that there could be no possible doubt ... The sticky grey mud in which the timbers were embedded had formed after 9000 BC in a post-Ice Age environment of mudflats, protected from the sea by sand and gravel barriers. The mudflats were dissected by numerous creeks and ponds filled with fresh or slightly salty water. We still don't know how far out in the current North Sea those barriers were, but the evidence would suggest some distance – perhaps a kilometre or more. Over the years

the barriers have been pushed back to their present position by the steady rise of post-Ice Age sea levels. This happened in a series of events, in which the barrier would be breached, the sea would pass through and another barrier would reform a little further inland. This process has never stopped, which is the main reason why the timbers were at such grave risk of destruction.'

7   See Pryor, ibid., p. 252: 'The place was always remote, marginal and, to use that word again, *liminal*. It was in every respect an ideal spot at which to undergo a rite of passage, whether one was living or dead.'

8   See Pryor, ibid., p. 270.

9   Ibid., p. 275.

10   Ibid., p. 275.

11   Andrew Brown, *Fishing in Utopia: Sweden and the Future that Disappeared*, p. 176.

Chapter One: Certainty

1   In Haiti, for example, elements of the Vodou religion have at times been incorporated into the Catholic mass, while in Cuba many practitioners of the Yoruba-originating belief system Santería see themselves also as good Catholics. Yet syncretic Catholic folk religion is anathema to many Protestant evangelicals.

2   'The real division today is not between believers and non-believers. Rather, it is between those who see violence as the solution to the world's problems, and those who recognise the urgent need for a more just and peaceful international order.' Tina Beattie, *The New Atheists*, p. 94.

3   Richard Dawkins, *The God Delusion*, p. 15.

4   Ibid., p. 185.

5   Ibid., p. 348

6   Christopher Hitchens, *God is Not Great*, p. 52, where Hitchens catalogues a variety of disagreeable practices which he associates with scriptural tradition.

7   Which negativises the prayerful Muslim expression of devotion, or *takbir: Allahu Akbar*, 'God is Great'.

8   Ibid., p. 125.

9   Ibid., p. 125.

10   Ibid., p. 125.

11   See Sophie Elmhirst, 'Is Richard Dawkins destroying his reputation?' in 'The Long Read', *Guardian*, 9 June 2015.

12   For some of the recent literature, see chapter 4 of *The God Delusion*, 'Why there almost certainly is no God'; Keith Ward, *The Evidence for God*, passim; and Alistair McGrath and Joanna Collicutt McGrath, *The Dawkins Delusion?*, passim. See also Tina Beattie, ibid., chapter

2 'The Man of Science and his religious others', pp. 39–56 for an excellent and nuanced discussion of the rise of the scientific world-view and misunderstandings by New Atheists like Richard Dawkins and Christopher Hitchens of the origins and social functions of religion.

13 See Ken Sengupta, 'Meet the men taking up arms to protect the Middle East's ancient treasures', *Spectator*, 12 September 2015: 'John Curtis, the keeper of the British Museum's Ancient Near East department, visited Babylon at the invitation of Iraqi colleagues and said what had happened was "tantamount to establishing a military camp around the Great Pyramid in Egypt or around Stonehenge in Britain". The US countered that the looting at Babylon would have been worse had they not been there at all. Now, in another country and another war, my friends among the Syrian rebels ask: why did the US-led coalition not do more to protect Palmyra? There were daily bulletins of the Isis advance on the city and warnings of the certain destruction of the Unesco world heritage site if they managed to capture it. But no air strikes took place to stop the jihadists.'

14 Which was frequently much less censorious in matters of religion than the modern one.

15 Ed Pilkington, *Guardian*, 8 December 2015: 'Donald Trump: Ban all Muslims entering US'.

16 For an excellent discussion of Kant's thinking on religion and God see Terry F. Godlove, *Kant and the Meaning of Religion*, especially p. 164: 'Kant sees deeply into our inability to give sense to "God" in the way that we do ordinary empirical concepts. He sees that finite creatures cannot somehow leverage the logical and material relationships between earth-bound concepts so as to refer to something not similarly bound. Here is Kant the all-destroyer. But here, too, we come to a turning-point. For even having so thoroughly scorched the semantic earth, still, God-talk is not, for Kant, bogus in the way that talk of fortune or faith is.'

17 Graeme Smith, *A Short History of Secularism*, pp. 2–3.

18 Ibid., p. 9.

19 Though Tim Whitmarsh, in his recent book *Battling the Gods*, has argued plausibly that 'disbelief in the supernatural is as old as the hills' (p. 4). Whitmarsh thinks atheism has a long and distinguished history, a history 'at least as old as the monotheistic religions of Abraham' (p. 7), but whose evidence is complex and elusive. 'It is very hard', he writes, 'to locate the atheists in many ancient cultures' (p. 7). Nevertheless, the author's fascinating history of views and opinions that he says have been 'airbrushed out of ancient history' focuses by his own admission on 'a relatively small segment of

ancient society ... educated males from the upper tiers of Greek and Roman life' (p. 8), which may not be fully representative of the mainstream of antique society.

20   Gavin Hyman, *A Short History of Atheism*, p. xvii.
21   Ibid., p. 180. See also Fergus Kerr, *Immortal Longings*, pp. 182–4, for Kerr's nuanced discussion of Rahner and the incomprehensibility of God.
22   Hyman, ibid., p. 180.
23   Quoted by Hyman, ibid., p. 118.
24   Peter Hitchens, *The Rage Against God*, pp. 160–1.
25   Tina Beattie, ibid., p. 79.
26   See Amira K. Bennison, *The Great Caliphs*, for a splendid account of the diverse and cosmopolitan 'Abbasid world. As Bennison shows, this was a pluralistic society which fully recognised ethnic and religious differences and where 'Christians, Jews and Zoroastrians were allowed to practise their faiths as religious minorities' (p. 7). She argues furthermore that the 'Abbasid caliphs saw themselves as the intellectual and cultural inheritors of the Mediterranean empires that had preceded them, including those of Greece, Rome and Persia.
27   George Steiner, *Real Presences*, p. 225.
28   Ibid., pp. 226–7.
29   Peter Hitchens, *The Rage Against God*, pp. 13–14.
30   See Hooton, ibid., p. 63: 'This building was likely to have been a chapel next to the channel leading to Cley, inhabited by a holy man, whose sole task was to provide such a service. It may well have been occupied by Robert de Berton Benedich, who was mentioned in a document of 1343. In it he was described as a "chaplain, and Hermit of Cleye by Blakeney Haven by the sea"'.
31   See Hooton, ibid., p. 61, 'The flint and brick structure to the left may have been the site of a shrine containing the image of the Virgin Mary that was mentioned in the will of John Symonds of Cley who died in 1502.'
32   Hyman, ibid., p. 50.
33   Rowan Williams, *Writing in the Dust*, passim.
34   See Denys Turner, *The Darkness of God*, p. 18.
35   *The Life of Moses*, Book Two, ii, The Second Theophany: The Ascent of Mount Sinai, Ex. 20:18–21, p. 16, in *The Essential Writings of Christian Mysticism*, ed. Bernard McGinn.
36   See Denys Turner, ibid., p. 264, quoting Bernard McGinn, who in turn is quoting Simone Weil.
37   Julia Blackburn, *The Leper's Companions*, pp. 12–13.
38   See Hyman, p. 17: 'Outright atheism remains a minority confession.'

39 Donated in 1450 by Johannis Goldale and his wife Katherine, and perhaps the best preserved in the country, its panels depict the donors and the 'four doctors' of the Church: SS Ambrose, Gregory, Jerome and Augustine.

40 See Philip Toynbee, *Part of a Journey*, p. 52.

Chapter Two: Doubt

1 See Eamon Duffy, *The Stripping of the Altars*, pp. 5–6: 'I have tried to demonstrate the anxiety of the Elizabethan episcopate about the persistence and vitality of the forms of traditional religion, an anxiety reflected in the determination with which they set themselves to achieve the destruction of them.'

2 See Andy Wood, 'Kett's Rebellion' in *Medieval Norwich*, ed. Carole Rawcliffe and Richard Wilson, p. 291: 'The Reformation heightened such conflicts. The Dissolution of the Monasteries and the radical changes to church ornaments and services were often understood as attempts by the "gentlemen" to destroy the cultural and spiritual basis of plebeian community, at the same time as their aggressive seigneurialism undercut its material basis.'

3 The identity of Richeldis (Latin) or Richelde (French) is somewhat mysterious: her name is usually given in Latin form, probably for legal purposes in official documents.

4 See Marzac-Holland, ibid., p. 38 for the history of the shrine's founder, her Norman background and the two places, Faverches in the region of Saint Lô and modern *département* of Manches, and Fervaques, eight miles from Orbec, which can plausibly lay claim to be her place of origin.

5 Thought to be the sole reliable source of our knowledge of Richelde, of which one copy (believed to be the only one in existence) is deposited in the Pepys Library of Magdalene College, Cambridge.

6 Marzac-Holland, ibid., p. 3.

7 Bernard Phillips, 'The Paper', May 1983 edition.

8 Marzac-Holland, ibid., p. 19.

9 Ibid., p. 25.

10 Ibid., p. 26.

11 See Victor Gollancz and Barbara Greene, *God of a Hundred Names*, pp. 204–5

12 See *The Cambridge Companion to Medieval English Mysticism*, 'c. 1080–1215: texts', by Henrietta Leyser p. 53.

13 Denys Turner, *The Darkness of God*, p. 4.

14 Bernard McGinn, *The Essential Writings of Christian Mysticism*, p. xv.

15 Bernard McGinn, ibid., p. xv.

16 McGinn, ibid., p. 348.

17 McGinn, ibid., p. 347.

18 McGinn, ibid., p. 266.
19 *The Dark Night of the Soul*, Book II, chapter 5, ibid., p. 386.
20 Quoted in McGinn, ibid., p. 365.
21 Mt. 27:46, quoted in McGinn, ibid., p. 376.
22 I am indebted for this quotation to Dr Edward Howells of Heythrop College, London.
23 Bernard McGinn has coined for this sense of abandonment the apt phrase 'mystical dereliction'; and I am indebted also to him for his generous advice on this topic.
24 See John D. Caputo, *Heidegger and Aquinas*, p. 276.
25 Ibid., p. 276.
26 For clarification of what Eckhart is getting at, see Caputo, ibid., p. 276: '"God" is everything we say of Him, whereas the Godhead remains behind, its essential Being untouched by this discourse. For if "God" is Father, Son, and Spirit, causa prima, creator, omniscient and omnipotent, then the Godhead is none of these things; it is *prior* to these things, deeper, not yet manifest, the concealed *Wesen*, the *Ab-wesen*, in the manifest God (*An-wesen*). All the names of "God", whether they are drawn from philosophy or faith, metaphysics or theology, fall short of the divine abyss.'
27 Ibid., p. 276.
28 Nicholas Watson, 'Introduction', *The Cambridge Companion to Medieval English Mysticism*, p. 5.
29 Ibid., p. 6.
30 McGinn, ibid., p. 390.
31 McGinn, ibid., p. 392.
32 Quotation from the author's original book proposal to I.B. Tauris.
33 *Theological Investigations* 4, p. 180 ff., quoted in Fergus Kerr, *Immortal Longings*, p. 174.
34 W. H. Vanstone, *The Stature of Waiting*, p. 83.
35 Ursula Le Guin, *The Left Hand of Darkness*, p. 188.
36 See Barbara J. Bucknell, *Ursula K. LeGuin*, p. 74: 'The Gethenian myths and legends illustrate … the interrelatedness of left and right, light and darkness, shadow and snow, birth and death, revelation and ignorance, beginning and end, and the denial of beginning and end.'
37 See Bucknell, ibid., p. 68: 'Towards the end of Genly's and Estraven's journey across the ice, the yin-yang symbolism is explained. Genly draws the ancient Chinese symbol of the double curve inside a circle, one half white and the other black. The white side stands for the yang principle, which is light, masculine and active. The black side stands for the yin principle, which is dark, feminine and receptive … Repeating a line from an old Gethenian poem that Estraven had quoted to him earlier in their journey, Genly says:

"Light is the left hand of darkness ... how did it go? Light, dark. Fear, courage. Cold, warmth. Female, male. It is yourself, Therem. Both and one. A shadow on snow."'

38 Ibid., p. 68.
39 See Bucknell, ibid., p. 69: 'The Handdara cult bears a very strong resemblance to Taoism. The darkness it cultivates is the darkness of mystery, beyond all answers and solutions. As the Taoist places the highest value on the Void, the adept of the Handdara gives praise "to Darkness and Creation unfinished" and studies how to achieve ignorance.'
40 Ursula Le Guin, *The Left Hand of Darkness*, p. 6.
41 Ibid., p. 65.
42 Ibid., pp. 65–6.

Chapter Three: Endurance

1   John Cowper Powys, *Wolf Solent*, p. 151.
2   Ibid., p. 151.
3   Ibid., p. 151.
4   Wiveton, Cley, Blakeney (or formerly 'Snitterley'), Salthouse and Wells.
5   Nicholas Comfort, *The Lost City of Dunwich*, p. vi.
6   Neil R. Storey, *The Lost Coast of Norfolk*, p. 67.
7   Ibid., p. 63.
8   Ibid., p. 63.
9   Ibid., p. 70: 'Fate and his unique blend of personal gallantry, tenacity and leadership of his crews has marked him out as the greatest of all the lifeboatmen; he was, as his memorial states, simply "one of the bravest men who ever lived".'
10 Julia Blackburn, *Threads*, p. 11.
11 Ibid., p. 278.
12 Ibid., p. 327.
13 Ibid., p. 336.
14 Ibid., p. 336.
15 In his early novel *Rodmoor* (1916), which – unusually for Powys – conjures the blustery eastern coast rather than that of Wessex.
16 John Cowper Powys, *Rodmoor* pp. 349–50.
17 G. Wilson Knight, *The Saturnian Quest*, p. 24.
18 Ibid., p. 24.
19 See Eamon Duffy, *Marking the Hours*, p. 5: 'The principal contents of the Book of Hours were in fact originally private devotions which had, by the twelfth century, become a routine and often obligatory extension of the Monastic round of worship, or *Opus Dei*. Monks and canons (clerics living in community under a rule) were obliged to the weekly recitation recited of more or less the entire Psalter in

a complex arrangement divided into the seven major daily offices of Matins (or "Vigils", originally recited in the night), Lauds (the dawn office), Prime, Terce, Sext and Nones (the shorter "day" offices), Vespers (the evening office) plus the short bed-time service of Compline.'

20 Eamon Duffy, ibid., p. 68.

21 Ibid., p. 64.

22 Ibid., p. 64.

23 A prayer-cycle of the Canonical Hours which mark the divisions of the day into fixed periods for prayer and worship. In the Catholic Church it is still read on All Souls Day for souls in Purgatory.

24 Ibid., p. 69.

25 Ibid., p. 69.

26 Graeme Smith, *A Short History of Secularism*, p. 8.

27 Ibid., p. 13.

28 Stephen Mitchell, *A Book of Psalms*, Psalm 13, p. 6.

29 Revised Standard Version, Psalm 137: verses 1–5.

30 J. L. Carr, *A Month in the Country*, p. 86.

31 Mervyn Peake puts it well, and more simply, in his novel *Titus Alone*, p. 197: 'There is nothing we can do, except live.'

32 Situated in some of the loveliest countryside in north Norfolk, Binham Priory was a Norman and Benedictine foundation. Established around 1091 by Peter de Valoines, head of a prominent baronial family who came over to England with Duke William at the Conquest, the priory church was a monastic dependency of St Albans. The West Front is of special architectural interest and may boast the earliest surviving example of bar tracery – invented in Reims Cathedral – in England. Pevsner (p. 390) suggests that 'the Binham window must have been very beautiful when it was intact and without the brick infill.'

33 It is an image used, with great appropriateness on the cover of Eamon Duffy's book *The Stripping of the Altars*.

34 Stephen Mitchell, ibid., Psalm 102, p. 48.

35 Sylvain Tesson, *Consolations of the Forest*, p. 192.

36 Ibid., p. 192.

37 Ibid., pp. 42–3.

38 Ibid., p. 93.

39 Ursula Le Guin, *The Tombs of Atuan*, p. 149. In this second novel of the Earthsea cycle, situated in and below the sprawling temple complex of the island of Atuan, the priestess Arha ('the Eaten One', who is able in the end to reclaim her given name, Tenar) lives in darkness, deep within an underground maze of tunnels, in lifelong servitude to the Nameless Ones: the malignant and hidden powers of Earthsea. But Tenar chooses to leave Atuan in the Kargad

Lands with the wizard Ged, and sail west to Havnor, so opting for freedom over vassalage, light over darkness. Le Guin writes thus, and with characteristically terse wisdom, of Tenar's release from enslavement: 'A dark hand had let go its lifelong hold upon her heart. But she did not feel joy, as she had in the mountains. She put her head down in her arms and cried, and her cheeks were salt and wet. She cried for the waste of her years in bondage to a useless evil. She wept in pain, because she was free' (ibid., p. 149).

Chapter Four: Revival

1   Revised Standard Version, Ecclesiastes 3: 1–6.
2   Ursula Le Guin, *The Farthest Shore*, p. 131.
3   Paul Kocher, *Master of Middle-earth: The Achievement of J.R.R. Tolkien in Fiction*, p. 82.
4   Ibid., p. 82.
5   Ibid., p. 92.
6   Milan Kundera, *Ignorance*, p. 121.
7   Andrew Brown, *Fishing in Utopia*, p. 78.
8   Ibid. p. 117.
9   Ibid. p. 118.
10   Philip Toynbee, *Part of a Journey*, p. 315.
11   Rainer Maria Rilke, *Duino Elegies*, ed. and trans. Stephen Mitchell, p. 61.
12   Charles Tomlinson, 'Far Point', *Annunciations*, p. 23.
13   Ibid., p. 24.
14   John Bowker, *The Meanings of Death*, p. 216: 'It is not possible to arrive at life except via the route of death ... It is not possible to acquire new energy out of nowhere from nothing.'
15   J. R. R. Tolkien, *The Lord of the Rings*, p. 1067.
16   Graeme Smith, *A Short History of Secularism*, pp. 14–15: 'One feature of contemporary Western society is the failure of atheism. The numbers of those who identify themselves as atheists or who belong to organisations such as the Secular Society or the American Humanist Association are extremely low. *The European Values Study* for 1999/2000 reported than on average 5 per cent of Europeans identified themselves as atheists.'
17   Rory MacLean, *Falling for Icarus*, p. 329.
18   Ibid., p. 330.
19   Ibid., p. 331.
20   See Keith Ward, *The Evidence for God*, p. 18: 'I want to say that art is evidence, both strong and plentiful, for a transcendent dimension, for the existence of objective value and meaning. But the evidence will not be compelling for everyone. Some people will deny that it is evidence at all, especially if they think that all values are just

subjective reactions to objective neutral facts. This disagreement cannot be theoretically resolved. It reveals a fundamental gulf between diverse ways of seeing human experience, and human knowledge of reality. There is no neutrally available evidence that will bridge that gulf.'

21   Ibid., p. 17: 'For some people, such appreciation is the most important thing in their lives. We may say 'Art is their religion'. But it is, taken on its own, a rather odd sort of religion. It often lacks any very obvious moral or intellectual dimension. It concentrates on feeling rather than on morally responsible action or a great interest in consistency and coherence of thought. We do not expect great artists to be saints or sages. But they have insights into human existence which reveal things many of us would not otherwise have known.'

22   Philip Toynbee, *Part of a Journey*, p. 143.

23   Though the association of Simonetta with the painting has been disputed, by for example Felipe Fernández-Armesto.

24   Richard Burns, *Sandro and Simonetta*, p. 204.

25   Ibid., p. 206.

26   See Mike Petty, 'Richard Burns: Obituary', *Independent*, 3 September 1992

27   Depression seems to prey disproportionately on great writers. See Nicholas Wroe, 'England's Time Lord', *Guardian*, 16 October 2004, an illuminating piece on Alan Garner, who has battled all his life with bipolar disorder: 'Several sessions with a psychiatrist got him back to work but there were periodic episodes over the years until, in 1980, he says, "it was as if the lights were turned down and I lost all sense of worth". He remembers listening to Benjamin Britten's Serenade for tenor and horn. "I had to leave the room because I thought it would kill me. For two years I spent 12 hours a day lying on the settle in the kitchen, and the other 12 hours in bed. How my family survived I do not know. The only people who connected with me were Joseph and Elizabeth, who were infants, and they acted like animals and stroked the back of my neck. After two years it went quicker than any aspirin could shift a headache and I thought what on earth was all that about?"'.

28   Ibid., p. 249.

29   Ursula Le Guin, *The Dispossessed*, p. 277.

30   Ibid., p. 277.

31   Penelope Lively, *Moon Tiger*, p. 206.

32   Ibid., p. 207.

Notes

Conclusion: Return

1 W. H. Vanstone, *The Stature of Waiting*, p. 103.
2 See Gavin Hyman on Richard Swinburne, ibid., p. 63.
3 George Steiner, *Real Presences*, pp. 226–7.
4 Philip Toynbee, *Part of a Journey*, p. 46.
5 The sublime cinematography of Ward's film *Map of the Human Heart* (1993) uses the untamed wilderness of the Canadian Arctic as a vivid metaphor for the doomed love of an Eskimo boy, Avik (Jason Scott Lee), for a mixed-race (half Apache, half white) girl called Albertine (Anne Parillaud) with whom he falls in love as a child.
6 Played with immense sensitivity by Kristin Scott Thomas.
7 The 'Cave of Swimmers' exists in fact, though the plot of both the novel and film *The English Patient* is mostly fictional. The cave was discovered in the Gilf Kebir plateau of the Libyan Desert by the Hungarian explorer László Almásy in October 1933.
8 *The English Patient* (dir. Anthony Minghella, 1996).

BIBLIOGRAPHY

Beattie, Tina, *The New Atheists: The Twilight of Reason and the War on Religion*, London, Darton, Longman and Todd, 2007

Blackburn, Julia, *The Leper's Companions*, London, Jonathan Cape, 1999
– *Threads: The Delicate Life of John Craske*, London, Jonathan Cape, 2015

Book of Margery Kempe, The, edited with an introduction by B. A. Windeatt, London, Folio Society, 2014

Bennison, Amira K., *The Great Caliphs: The Golden Age of the Abbasid Empire*, London, I.B.Tauris, 2009

Bowker, John, *The Meanings of Death*, Cambridge, Cambridge University Press, 1991

Brown, Andrew, *Fishing in Utopia: Sweden and the Future that Disappeared*, London, Granta, 2008

Bucknell, Barbara J., *Ursula K. LeGuin*, New York, Frederick Ungar Publishing, 1981

Burns, Richard, *Sandro and Simonetta*, London, Bloomsbury, 1992

Caputo, John D., *Heidegger and Aquinas: An Essay on Overcoming Metaphysics*, New York, Fordham University Press, 1982

Carr, J. L., *A Month in the Country*, London, Penguin, 2000

Cloud of Unknowing, The, edited by Emilie Griffin, Mawhah, Paulist Press, 1981

Comfort, Nicholas, *The Lost City of Dunwich*, Lavenham, Terence Dalton, 1994

Crossley-Holland, Kevin, *Poems from East Anglia*, London, Enitharmon Press, 1997

Dawkins, Richard, *The God Delusion*, London, Bantam Press, 2006

Duffy, Eamon, *The Stripping of the Altars: Traditional Religion in England c.1400-c.1580*, New Haven, Yale University Press, 1992
– *Marking the Hours: English People and their Prayers 1240-1570*, New Haven, Yale University Press, 2006

Fanous, Samuel and Gillespie, Vincent, *The Cambridge Companion to Medieval English Mysticism*, Cambridge, Cambridge University Press, 2011

Godlove, Terry F., *Kant and the Meaning of Religion: The Critical Philosophy and Modern Religious Thought*, London, I.B.Tauris, 2014

Greene, Barbara and Gollancz, Victor, *God of a Hundred Names*, London, Victor Gollancz, 1962

Hitchens, Christopher, *God is Not Great: How Religion Poisons Everything*, London, Atlantic, 2007

Hitchens, Peter, *The Rage Against God*, London, Bloomsbury, 2010

Hooton, Jonathan, *The Glaven Ports: A Maritime History of Blakeney, Cley and Wiveton in North Norfolk*, Blakeney, Blakeney History Group, 1996

Housman, A. E., *A Shropshire Lad*, London, Harrap, 1953

Hyman, Gavin, *A Short History of Atheism*, London, I.B.Tauris, 2010

Julian of Norwich, *Revelations of Divine Love*, trans. by Elizabeth Spearing, introduction by A. C. Spearing, London, Penguin, 1998

Kerr, Fergus, *Immortal Longings: Versions of Transcending Humanity*, London, SPCK, 1997

Kocher, Paul, *Master of Middle-earth: The Achievement of J. R. R. Tolkien in Fiction*, London, Penguin, 1972

Kundera, Milan, *Ignorance*, London, Faber and Faber, 2002

Le Guin, Ursula, *The Dispossessed*, St Albans, Granada, 1975
  – *The Farthest Shore*, London, Victor Gollancz, 1973
  – *The Left Hand of Darkness*, London, Futura, 1981
  – *The Tombs of Atuan*, London, Victor Gollancz, 1972

Lively, Penelope, *Moon Tiger*, London, Andre Deutsch, 1987

Marzac-Holland, Nicole, *Three Norfolk Mystics: Richelde de Faverches in Walsingham, Julian, Recluse in Norwich, Margery Kempe in Lynn*, Burnham Market, C. J. & M. Isaacson, 1983

McGinn, Bernard, *The Essential Writings of Christian Mysticism*, New York, Random House, 2006

McGrath, Alistair and McGrath, Joanna Collicutt, *The Dawkins Delusion?: Atheist Fundamentalism and the Denial of the Divine*, London, SPCK, 2007

MacLean, Rory, *Falling for Icarus: A Journey among the Cretans*, London, Penguin, 2005

Mitchell, Stephen, *A Book of Psalms*, New York, HarperCollins, 1993
  – *The Selected Poetry of Rainer Maria Rilke*, New York, Random House, 1982

Ondaatje, Michael, *The English Patient*, London, Bloomsbury, 1992

Peake, Mervyn, *Titus Alone*, London, Penguin, 1970

Pevsner, Nikolaus and Wilson, Bill, *The Buildings of England, Norfolk 1: Norwich and North-East*, New Haven, Yale University Press, 2002

Powys, John Cowper, *A Glastonbury Romance*, London, Picador, 1980
  – *Rodmoor*, London, Faber and Faber, 2011
  – *Weymouth Sands*, London, Picador, 1980
  – *Wolf Solent*, London, Penguin, 1964

Bibliography

Pryor, Francis, *Seahenge: A Quest for Life and Death in Bronze Age Britain*, London, HarperCollins, 2001

Rawcliffe, Carole and Wilson, Richard, *Medieval Norwich*, London, Hambledon and London, 2004

Sail, Lawrence, *Songs of the Darkness: Poems for Christmas*, London, Enitharmon Press, 2010

Smith, Graeme, *A Short History of Secularism*, London, I.B.Tauris, 2007

Steiner, George, *Real Presences*, London, Faber and Faber, 1989

Storey, Neil R., *The Lost Coast of Norfolk*, Stroud, Sutton Publishing, 2006

Tesson, Sylvain, *Consolations of the Forest: Alone in a Cabin in the Middle Taiga*, London, Allen Lane, 2013

Thiemann, Ronald F., *The Humble Sublime: Secularity and the Politics of Belief*, London, I.B.Tauris, 2014

Tolkien, J. R. R., *The Lord of the Rings*, London, George Allen and Unwin, 1969

Toynbee, Philip, *Part of a Journey: An Autobiographical Journal 1977-79*, London, Fount, 1982

Turner, Denys, *The Darkness of God: Negativity and Christian Mysticism*, Cambridge, Cambridge University Press, 1995

Tomlinson, Charles, *Annunciations*, Oxford, Oxford University Press, 1989

Vanstone, W. H., *The Stature of Waiting*, London, Darton, Longman and Todd, 1982

Ward, Keith, *The Evidence for God: The Case for the Existence of the Spiritual Dimension*, London, Darton, Longman and Todd, 2014

Whitmarsh, Tim, *Battling the Gods: Atheism in the Ancient World*, London, Faber, 2016

Williams, Rowan, *Writing in the Dust: Reflections on 11th September and its Aftermath*, London, Hodder and Stoughton, 2002

Wilson Knight, G., *The Saturnian Quest: A Chart of the Prose Works of John Cowper Powys*, London, Methuen, 1964

INDEX